B...
GRA...
Evangelis...
Alway...

Dear Friend,

I am pleased to send you this copy of *Words of Wisdom: A Journey Through Psalms and Proverbs* compiled by George M. Wilson, a member of my father's original team and a co-founder of the Billy Graham Evangelistic Association.

Mr. Wilson modeled this 31-day devotional on a Bible study formula my father used for years—five psalms and one chapter of Proverbs for each day. This method of study became a part of my father's devotions and was in addition to his daily Scripture reading. Our hope is that this book will bless you in your own Bible study and devotional time. My prayer for you as you read through *Words of Wisdom* is that *"through the encouragement of the Scriptures [you] might have hope"* (Romans 15:4, ESV).

For more than 60 years, the Billy Graham Evangelistic Association has worked to take the Good News of Jesus Christ throughout the world by every effective means, and I'm excited about what God will do in the years ahead.

We would appreciate knowing how our ministry has touched your life. May God richly bless you.

Sincerely,

Franklin Graham
President

If you would like to know more about our ministry, please contact us:

IN THE U.S.
Billy Graham Evangelistic Association
1 Billy Graham Parkway
Charlotte, NC 28201-0001
BillyGraham.org
info@bgea.org
Toll-free: 1-877-247-2426

IN CANADA
Billy Graham Evangelistic
   Association of Canada
20 Hopewell Way NE
Calgary, AB T3J 5H5
BillyGraham.ca
Toll-free: 1-888-393-0003

WORDS OF WISDOM

This special edition of *Words of Wisdom* is published by Tyndale for the Billy Graham Evangelistic Association.

BILLY
GRAHAM
Evangelistic Association

Always Good News.

Visit Tyndale online at www.tyndale.com.

Words of Wisdom: A Journey Through Psalms and Proverbs

All Scripture portions are taken from the *Holy Bible,* New Living Translation, copyright © 1996, 2004, 2007, 2013. Used by permission of Tyndale House Publishers, Inc., Carol Stream, Illinois 60188. All rights reserved.

Unless otherwise indicated, all Scripture quotations are taken from the *Holy Bible*, New Living Translation, copyright © 1996, 2004, 2007, 2013 by Tyndale House Foundation. Used by permission of Tyndale House Publishers, Inc., Carol Stream, Illinois 60188. All rights reserved.

Scripture quotations marked KJV are taken from the *Holy Bible,* King James Version.

Scripture quotations marked ESV are taken from *The Holy Bible,* English Standard Version® (ESV®), copyright © 2001 by Crossway, a publishing ministry of Good News Publishers. Used by permission. All rights reserved.

Scripture quotations marked NIV are taken from the Holy Bible, *New International Version,® NIV.®* Copyright © 1973, 1978, 1984, 2011 by Biblica, Inc.™ Used by permission of Zondervan. All rights reserved worldwide. www.zondervan.com.

Scripture quotations marked NKJV are taken from the New King James Version.® Copyright © 1982 by Thomas Nelson, Inc. Used by permission. All rights reserved.

Scripture quotations marked TLB are taken from *The Living Bible,* copyright © 1971 by Tyndale House Foundation. Used by permission of Tyndale House Publishers, Inc., Carol Stream, Illinois 60188. All rights reserved.

Use of content written by Mr. George M. Wilson, including Preface and Interpretive Note are copyrighted to Jean Wilson Greener, Judith Wilson Grimes Ph.D., and Janet Wilson Hanks, 2013. Used by permission.

TYNDALE and Tyndale's quill logo are registered trademarks of Tyndale House Publishers, Inc.

New Living Translation, NLT, and the New Living Translation logo are registered trademarks of Tyndale House Publishers, Inc.

ISBN-13: 978-1-4143-8001-8 Softcover

Printed in the United States of America

18 17 16 15 14 13
7   6   5   4   3   2   1

FOREWORD

The late Senator Everett Dirksen of Illinois once told me that one could not help but draw great inspiration from the reading of the Psalms and the Proverbs. For many years I have made it a practice to read five Psalms and a chapter of the book of Proverbs each day, aside from my other Bible reading and study, and it has been a great blessing to me.

By reading five Psalms and one chapter of Proverbs daily, you will be able to read them through each month. The Psalms will tell you how to get along with God, and the Proverbs will tell you how to get along with your fellowman. In Deuteronomy 6:5 we read, "Thou shalt love the Lord thy God with all thine heart, and with all thy soul, and with all thy might" (KJV). In Leviticus 19:18 we read, "Don't seek vengeance. Don't bear a grudge; but love your neighbor as yourself, for I am Jehovah" (TLB). Both of these great affirmations are underlined in the Psalms and Proverbs.

In this book you have a wonderful treat in store. May God bless you as you begin to live in its pages.

Billy Graham

PREFACE

In a way unmatched by any other literature, the book of Psalms draws us apart from the workaday life of man, brings us into the sanctuary, and directs us into precious communion with God. The Hebrew word for Psalms is *tehillim,* which in a general way means poems of praise composed to be sung.

The book of Psalms really gives us a summary of both the Old and New Testaments. All the way through the book, and particularly in the Messianic psalms, we find the message of the Christ to come. Our risen Lord referred to the Psalms in his last message before ascending to his Father. "When I was with you before, I told you that everything written about me . . . in the Psalms must be fulfilled" (Luke 24:44). In Colossians 3:16, the apostle Paul tells the believers, "Let the message about Christ, in all its richness, fill your lives. Teach and counsel each other with all the wisdom he gives. Sing psalms and hymns and spiritual songs to God with thankful hearts."

While the Psalms are all divinely inspired, they were composed at different times for different occasions, and have been put together rather independently of each other. King David was probably the author of most of the Psalms. In 2 Samuel 23:1 he is referred to as the "psalmist of Israel." One psalm (Psalm 90) was a prayer of Moses. Other psalms were written by Asaph, for in 2 Chronicles 29:30 Hezekiah ordered the Levites to "praise the LORD with the psalms written by David and by Asaph." The Chronicler also calls Asaph a seer, or prophet.

David's genius is found in his poetry. His lyrics became the Psalter for the early church of God. No other book, perhaps, is as helpful to a Christian's devotional life as is the book of Psalms.

The Psalms are divided into five sections, also called books. Each section concludes with "Amen and amen" or "Praise the LORD." The first section ends with Psalm 41; the second with Psalm 72; the third with Psalm 89; the fourth with Psalm 106. We have purposely not made these divisions in this devotional edition for the convenience of the reader using them for inspiration in his or her daily devotions.

George M. Wilson, 1913–1999
Executive Vice President,
Billy Graham Evangelistic Association, 1950–1987

DAY ONE

❦ PSALM 1

¹ Oh, the joys of those who do not
    follow the advice of the wicked,
    or stand around with sinners,
    or join in with mockers.
² But they delight in the law of the LORD,
    meditating on it day and night.
³ They are like trees planted along the riverbank,
    bearing fruit each season.
Their leaves never wither,
    and they prosper in all they do.

⁴ But not the wicked!
    They are like worthless chaff, scattered by
      the wind.
⁵ They will be condemned at the time of
      judgment.
Sinners will have no place among the godly.
⁶ For the LORD watches over the path of the godly,
    but the path of the wicked leads to
      destruction.

❧ PSALM 2

¹ Why are the nations so angry?
   Why do they waste their time with
      futile plans?
² The kings of the earth prepare for battle;
   the rulers plot together
 against the LORD
   and against his anointed one.
³ "Let us break their chains," they cry,
   "and free ourselves from slavery to God."

⁴ But the one who rules in heaven laughs.
   The Lord scoffs at them.
⁵ Then in anger he rebukes them,
   terrifying them with his fierce fury.
⁶ For the Lord declares, "I have placed my chosen
      king on the throne
   in Jerusalem, on my holy mountain."

⁷ The king proclaims the LORD's decree:
 "The LORD said to me, 'You are my son.
   Today I have become your Father.
⁸ Only ask, and I will give you the nations as your
      inheritance,
   the whole earth as your possession.

⁹ You will break them with an iron rod
   and smash them like clay pots.'"

¹⁰ Now then, you kings, act wisely!
   Be warned, you rulers of the earth!
¹¹ Serve the LORD with reverent fear,
   and rejoice with trembling.
¹² Submit to God's royal son, or he will become angry,
   and you will be destroyed in the midst of all your
      activities—
   for his anger flares up in an instant.
   But what joy for all who take refuge in him!

🕊 PSALM 3

A psalm of David, regarding the time David fled from his son Absalom.

¹ O LORD, I have so many enemies;
   so many are against me.
² So many are saying,
   "God will never rescue him!"   *Interlude*

³ But you, O LORD, are a shield around me;
   you are my glory, the one who holds my head high.
⁴ I cried out to the LORD,
   and he answered me from his holy mountain.
                                                  Interlude

⁵ I lay down and slept,
    yet I woke up in safety,
    for the LORD was watching over me.
⁶ I am not afraid of ten thousand enemies
    who surround me on every side.

⁷ Arise, O LORD!
    Rescue me, my God!
  Slap all my enemies in the face!
    Shatter the teeth of the wicked!
⁸ Victory comes from you, O LORD.
    May you bless your people.   *Interlude*

🔥 PSALM 4

For the choir director: A psalm of David, to be accompanied by stringed instruments.

¹ Answer me when I call to you,
    O God who declares me innocent.
  Free me from my troubles.
    Have mercy on me and hear my prayer.

² How long will you people ruin my reputation?
    How long will you make groundless
        accusations?
    How long will you continue your lies?   *Interlude*

³ You can be sure of this:
  The LORD set apart the godly for himself.
  The LORD will answer when I call to him.

⁴ Don't sin by letting anger control you.
  Think about it overnight and remain silent.

Interlude

⁵ Offer sacrifices in the right spirit,
  and trust the LORD.

⁶ Many people say, "Who will show us better times?"
  Let your face smile on us, LORD.

⁷ You have given me greater joy
  than those who have abundant harvests of grain
    and new wine.

⁸ In peace I will lie down and sleep,
  for you alone, O LORD, will keep me safe.

❦ PSALM 5

For the choir director: A psalm of David, to be accompanied by the flute.

¹ O LORD, hear me as I pray;
  pay attention to my groaning.

² Listen to my cry for help, my King and my God,
  for I pray to no one but you.

³ Listen to my voice in the morning, LORD.

Each morning I bring my requests to you
  and wait expectantly.

4 O God, you take no pleasure in wickedness;
  you cannot tolerate the sins of the wicked.
5 Therefore, the proud may not stand in your
    presence,
  for you hate all who do evil.
6 You will destroy those who tell lies.
  The LORD detests murderers and deceivers.

7 Because of your unfailing love, I can enter your
    house;
  I will worship at your Temple with deepest awe.
8 Lead me in the right path, O LORD,
  or my enemies will conquer me.
Make your way plain for me to follow.

9 My enemies cannot speak a truthful word.
  Their deepest desire is to destroy others.
Their talk is foul, like the stench from an open grave.
  Their tongues are filled with flattery.
10 O God, declare them guilty.
  Let them be caught in their own traps.
Drive them away because of their many sins,
  for they have rebelled against you.

¹¹ But let all who take refuge in you rejoice;
    let them sing joyful praises forever.
  Spread your protection over them,
    that all who love your name may be filled
      with joy.
¹² For you bless the godly, O LORD;
    you surround them with your shield of love.

✳ PROVERBS 1

These are the proverbs of Solomon, David's son, king
of Israel.

² Their purpose is to teach people wisdom and
    discipline,
  to help them understand the insights of
    the wise.
³ Their purpose is to teach people to live disciplined
    and successful lives,
  to help them do what is right, just, and fair.
⁴ These proverbs will give insight to the simple,
  knowledge and discernment to the young.

⁵ Let the wise listen to these proverbs and become
    even wiser.
  Let those with understanding receive guidance

⁶ by exploring the meaning in these proverbs
and parables,
the words of the wise and their riddles.

⁷ Fear of the LORD is the foundation of true
knowledge,
but fools despise wisdom and discipline.

⁸ My child, listen when your father corrects you.
Don't neglect your mother's instruction.
⁹ What you learn from them will crown you with
grace
and be a chain of honor around your neck.

¹⁰ My child, if sinners entice you,
turn your back on them!
¹¹ They may say, "Come and join us.
Let's hide and kill someone!
Just for fun, let's ambush the innocent!
¹² Let's swallow them alive, like the grave;
let's swallow them whole, like those who go
down to the pit of death.
¹³ Think of the great things we'll get!
We'll fill our houses with all the stuff we take.
¹⁴ Come, throw in your lot with us;
we'll all share the loot."

¹⁵ My child, don't go along with them!
    Stay far away from their paths.
¹⁶ They rush to commit evil deeds.
    They hurry to commit murder.
¹⁷ If a bird sees a trap being set,
    it knows to stay away.
¹⁸ But these people set an ambush for themselves;
    they are trying to get themselves killed.
¹⁹ Such is the fate of all who are greedy for money;
    it robs them of life.

²⁰ Wisdom shouts in the streets.
    She cries out in the public square.
²¹ She calls to the crowds along the main street,
    to those gathered in front of the city gate:
²² "How long, you simpletons,
    will you insist on being simpleminded?
  How long will you mockers relish your mocking?
  How long will you fools hate knowledge?
²³ Come and listen to my counsel.
  I'll share my heart with you
    and make you wise.

²⁴ "I called you so often, but you wouldn't come.
    I reached out to you, but you paid no attention.

25 You ignored my advice
    and rejected the correction I offered.
26 So I will laugh when you are in trouble!
    I will mock you when disaster overtakes you—
27 when calamity overtakes you like a storm,
    when disaster engulfs you like a cyclone,
    and anguish and distress overwhelm you.

28 "When they cry for help, I will not answer.
    Though they anxiously search for me, they
        will not find me.
29 For they hated knowledge
    and chose not to fear the LORD.
30 They rejected my advice
    and paid no attention when I corrected them.
31 Therefore, they must eat the bitter fruit of living
        their own way,
    choking on their own schemes.
32 For simpletons turn away from me—to death.
    Fools are destroyed by their own complacency.
33 But all who listen to me will live in peace,
    untroubled by fear of harm."

DAY TWO

🔥 PSALM 6

For the choir director: A psalm of David, to be accompanied by an eight-stringed instrument.

¹ O LORD, don't rebuke me in your anger
  or discipline me in your rage.
² Have compassion on me, LORD, for I am weak.
  Heal me, LORD, for my bones are in agony.
³ I am sick at heart.
  How long, O LORD, until you restore me?

⁴ Return, O LORD, and rescue me.
  Save me because of your unfailing love.
⁵ For the dead do not remember you.
  Who can praise you from the grave?

⁶ I am worn out from sobbing.
  All night I flood my bed with weeping,
    drenching it with my tears.
⁷ My vision is blurred by grief;
  my eyes are worn out because of all my
    enemies.

⁸ Go away, all you who do evil,
  for the LORD has heard my weeping.

⁹ The LORD has heard my plea;
   the LORD will answer my prayer.
¹⁰ May all my enemies be disgraced and terrified.
   May they suddenly turn back in shame.

🔥 PSALM 7

A psalm of David, which he sang to the LORD concerning Cush of the tribe of Benjamin.

¹ I come to you for protection, O LORD my God.
   Save me from my persecutors—rescue me!
² If you don't, they will maul me like a lion,
   tearing me to pieces with no one to rescue me.
³ O LORD my God, if I have done wrong
   or am guilty of injustice,
⁴ if I have betrayed a friend
   or plundered my enemy without cause,
⁵ then let my enemies capture me.
   Let them trample me into the ground
   and drag my honor in the dust.   *Interlude*

⁶ Arise, O LORD, in anger!
   Stand up against the fury of my enemies!
   Wake up, my God, and bring justice!
⁷ Gather the nations before you.
   Rule over them from on high.

⁸   The Lord judges the nations.
  Declare me righteous, O Lord,
      for I am innocent, O Most High!
⁹ End the evil of those who are wicked,
      and defend the righteous.
  For you look deep within the mind and heart,
      O righteous God.

¹⁰ God is my shield,
      saving those whose hearts are true and right.
¹¹ God is an honest judge.
      He is angry with the wicked every day.

¹² If a person does not repent,
      God will sharpen his sword;
      he will bend and string his bow.
¹³ He will prepare his deadly weapons
      and shoot his flaming arrows.

¹⁴ The wicked conceive evil;
      they are pregnant with trouble
      and give birth to lies.
¹⁵ They dig a deep pit to trap others,
      then fall into it themselves.
¹⁶ The trouble they make for others backfires
          on them.

The violence they plan falls on their own heads.

[17] I will thank the LORD because he is just;
     I will sing praise to the name of the LORD Most
     High.

🔥 PSALM 8

For the choir director: A psalm of David, to be accompanied by
a stringed instrument.

[1] O LORD, our Lord, your majestic name fills
     the earth!
     Your glory is higher than the heavens.
[2] You have taught children and infants
     to tell of your strength,
   silencing your enemies
     and all who oppose you.

[3] When I look at the night sky and see the work
     of your fingers—
     the moon and the stars you set in place—
[4] what are mere mortals that you should think about
     them,
     human beings that you should care for them?
[5] Yet you made them only a little lower than God
     and crowned them with glory and honor.

⁶ You gave them charge of everything you made,
    putting all things under their authority—
⁷ the flocks and the herds
    and all the wild animals,
⁸ the birds in the sky, the fish in the sea,
    and everything that swims the ocean currents.

⁹ O LORD, our Lord, your majestic name fills the
    earth!

❦ PSALM 9

*For the choir director: A psalm of David, to be sung to the tune
"Death of the Son."*

¹ I will praise you, LORD, with all my heart;
    I will tell of all the marvelous things you have
      done.
² I will be filled with joy because of you.
    I will sing praises to your name, O Most High.

³ My enemies retreated;
    they staggered and died when you appeared.
⁴ For you have judged in my favor;
    from your throne you have judged with fairness.
⁵ You have rebuked the nations and destroyed the
    wicked;
    you have erased their names forever.

⁶ The enemy is finished, in endless ruins;
　　the cities you uprooted are now forgotten.

⁷ But the LORD reigns forever,
　　executing judgment from his throne.
⁸ He will judge the world with justice
　　and rule the nations with fairness.
⁹ The LORD is a shelter for the oppressed,
　　a refuge in times of trouble.
¹⁰ Those who know your name trust in you,
　　for you, O LORD, do not abandon those who
　　　　search for you.

¹¹ Sing praises to the LORD who reigns in Jerusalem.
　　Tell the world about his unforgettable deeds.
¹² For he who avenges murder cares for the helpless.
　　He does not ignore the cries of those who suffer.

¹³ LORD, have mercy on me.
　　See how my enemies torment me.
　　Snatch me back from the jaws of death.
¹⁴ Save me so I can praise you publicly at Jerusalem's
　　　　gates,
　　so I can rejoice that you have rescued me.

¹⁵ The nations have fallen into the pit they dug for
　　　　others.

Their own feet have been caught in the trap
they set.

16 The Lord is known for his justice.
The wicked are trapped by their own deeds.

Quiet Interlude

17 The wicked will go down to the grave.
This is the fate of all the nations who ignore
God.

18 But the needy will not be ignored forever;
the hopes of the poor will not always be crushed.

19 Arise, O Lord!
Do not let mere mortals defy you!
Judge the nations!

20 Make them tremble in fear, O Lord.
Let the nations know they are merely human.

Interlude

❧ PSALM 10

1 O Lord, why do you stand so far away?
Why do you hide when I am in trouble?

2 The wicked arrogantly hunt down the poor.
Let them be caught in the evil they plan for
others.

³ For they brag about their evil desires;
  they praise the greedy and curse the LORD.

⁴ The wicked are too proud to seek God.
  They seem to think that God is dead.
⁵ Yet they succeed in everything they do.
  They do not see your punishment awaiting them.
  They sneer at all their enemies.
⁶ They think, "Nothing bad will ever happen to us!
  We will be free of trouble forever!"

⁷ Their mouths are full of cursing, lies, and threats.
  Trouble and evil are on the tips of their tongues.
⁸ They lurk in ambush in the villages,
  waiting to murder innocent people.
  They are always searching for helpless victims.
⁹ Like lions crouched in hiding,
  they wait to pounce on the helpless.
 Like hunters they capture the helpless
  and drag them away in nets.
¹⁰ Their helpless victims are crushed;
  they fall beneath the strength of the wicked.
¹¹ The wicked think, "God isn't watching us!
  He has closed his eyes and won't even see what
   we do!"

¹² Arise, O Lord!
   Punish the wicked, O God!
   Do not ignore the helpless!
¹³ Why do the wicked get away with despising God?
   They think, "God will never call us to account."
¹⁴ But you see the trouble and grief they cause.
   You take note of it and punish them.
   The helpless put their trust in you.
   You defend the orphans.

¹⁵ Break the arms of these wicked, evil people!
   Go after them until the last one is destroyed.
¹⁶ The Lord is king forever and ever!
   The godless nations will vanish from the land.
¹⁷ Lord, you know the hopes of the helpless.
   Surely you will hear their cries and comfort
      them.
¹⁸ You will bring justice to the orphans and the
      oppressed,
   so mere people can no longer terrify them.

✳ PROVERBS 2

¹ My child, listen to what I say,
   and treasure my commands.

² Tune your ears to wisdom,
    and concentrate on understanding.
³ Cry out for insight,
    and ask for understanding.
⁴ Search for them as you would for silver;
    seek them like hidden treasures.
⁵ Then you will understand what it means to fear
        the LORD,
    and you will gain knowledge of God.
⁶ For the LORD grants wisdom!
    From his mouth come knowledge and
        understanding.
⁷ He grants a treasure of common sense to the
        honest.
    He is a shield to those who walk with integrity.
⁸ He guards the paths of the just
    and protects those who are faithful to him.

⁹ Then you will understand what is right, just,
        and fair,
    and you will find the right way to go.
¹⁰ For wisdom will enter your heart,
    and knowledge will fill you with joy.
¹¹ Wise choices will watch over you.
    Understanding will keep you safe.

¹² Wisdom will save you from evil people,
  from those whose words are twisted.
¹³ These men turn from the right way
  to walk down dark paths.
¹⁴ They take pleasure in doing wrong,
  and they enjoy the twisted ways of evil.
¹⁵ Their actions are crooked,
  and their ways are wrong.

¹⁶ Wisdom will save you from the immoral woman,
  from the seductive words of the promiscuous
    woman.
¹⁷ She has abandoned her husband
  and ignores the covenant she made before God.
¹⁸ Entering her house leads to death;
  it is the road to the grave.
¹⁹ The man who visits her is doomed.
  He will never reach the paths of life.

²⁰ Follow the steps of good men instead,
  and stay on the paths of the righteous.
²¹ For only the godly will live in the land,
  and those with integrity will remain in it.
²² But the wicked will be removed from the land,
  and the treacherous will be uprooted.

DAY THREE

🔥 PSALM 11

For the choir director: A psalm of David.

¹ I trust in the LORD for protection.
  So why do you say to me,
    "Fly like a bird to the mountains for safety!
² The wicked are stringing their bows
    and fitting their arrows on the bowstrings.
  They shoot from the shadows
    at those whose hearts are right.
³ The foundations of law and order have collapsed.
    What can the righteous do?"

⁴ But the LORD is in his holy Temple;
    the LORD still rules from heaven.
  He watches everyone closely,
    examining every person on earth.
⁵ The LORD examines both the righteous and the
      wicked.
  He hates those who love violence.
⁶ He will rain down blazing coals and burning sulfur
      on the wicked,
    punishing them with scorching winds.

⁷ For the righteous LORD loves justice.
    The virtuous will see his face.

🔥 P S A L M 1 2

*For the choir director: A psalm of David, to be accompanied by an
eight-stringed instrument.*

¹ Help, O LORD, for the godly are fast disappearing!
    The faithful have vanished from the earth!
² Neighbors lie to each other,
    speaking with flattering lips and deceitful hearts.
³ May the LORD cut off their flattering lips
    and silence their boastful tongues.
⁴ They say, "We will lie to our hearts' content.
    Our lips are our own—who can stop us?"

⁵ The LORD replies, "I have seen violence done
        to the helpless,
    and I have heard the groans of the poor.
  Now I will rise up to rescue them,
    as they have longed for me to do."
⁶ The LORD's promises are pure,
    like silver refined in a furnace,
    purified seven times over.
⁷ Therefore, LORD, we know you will protect
        the oppressed,

preserving them forever from this lying
    generation,
8 even though the wicked strut about,
    and evil is praised throughout the land.

❦ PSALM 13

For the choir director: A psalm of David.

1 O LORD, how long will you forget me? Forever?
    How long will you look the other way?
2 How long must I struggle with anguish in
    my soul,
    with sorrow in my heart every day?
    How long will my enemy have the
    upper hand?

3 Turn and answer me, O LORD my God!
    Restore the sparkle to my eyes, or I will die.
4 Don't let my enemies gloat, saying, "We have
    defeated him!"
    Don't let them rejoice at my downfall.

5 But I trust in your unfailing love.
    I will rejoice because you have rescued me.
6 I will sing to the LORD
    because he is good to me.

🌿 PSALM 14

For the choir director: A psalm of David.

¹ Only fools say in their hearts,
    "There is no God."
  They are corrupt, and their actions are evil;
    not one of them does good!

² The LORD looks down from heaven
    on the entire human race;
  he looks to see if anyone is truly wise,
    if anyone seeks God.
³ But no, all have turned away;
    all have become corrupt.
  No one does good,
    not a single one!

⁴ Will those who do evil never learn?
    They eat up my people like bread
    and wouldn't think of praying to the LORD.
⁵ Terror will grip them,
    for God is with those who obey him.
⁶ The wicked frustrate the plans of the oppressed,
    but the LORD will protect his people.

⁷ Who will come from Mount Zion to rescue
      Israel?

When the LORD restores his people,
Jacob will shout with joy, and Israel will rejoice.

🌷 PSALM 15

A psalm of David.

¹ Who may worship in your sanctuary, LORD?
    Who may enter your presence on your holy hill?
² Those who lead blameless lives and do what is
        right,
    speaking the truth from sincere hearts.
³ Those who refuse to gossip
    or harm their neighbors
    or speak evil of their friends.
⁴ Those who despise flagrant sinners,
    and honor the faithful followers of the LORD,
    and keep their promises even when it hurts.
⁵ Those who lend money without charging interest,
    and who cannot be bribed to lie about the
        innocent.
  Such people will stand firm forever.

✳ PROVERBS 3

¹ My child, never forget the things I have taught you.
    Store my commands in your heart.

² If you do this, you will live many years,
   and your life will be satisfying.
³ Never let loyalty and kindness leave you!
   Tie them around your neck as a reminder.
   Write them deep within your heart.
⁴ Then you will find favor with both God and
      people,
   and you will earn a good reputation.

⁵ Trust in the LORD with all your heart;
   do not depend on your own understanding.
⁶ Seek his will in all you do,
   and he will show you which path to take.

⁷ Don't be impressed with your own wisdom.
   Instead, fear the LORD and turn away from evil.
⁸ Then you will have healing for your body
   and strength for your bones.

⁹ Honor the LORD with your wealth
   and with the best part of everything you
      produce.
¹⁰ Then he will fill your barns with grain,
   and your vats will overflow with good wine.

¹¹ My child, don't reject the LORD's discipline,
   and don't be upset when he corrects you.

¹² For the LORD corrects those he loves,
   just as a father corrects a child in whom
      he delights.

¹³ Joyful is the person who finds wisdom,
   the one who gains understanding.
¹⁴ For wisdom is more profitable than silver,
   and her wages are better than gold.
¹⁵ Wisdom is more precious than rubies;
   nothing you desire can compare with her.
¹⁶ She offers you long life in her right hand,
   and riches and honor in her left.
¹⁷ She will guide you down delightful paths;
   all her ways are satisfying.
¹⁸ Wisdom is a tree of life to those who embrace her;
   happy are those who hold her tightly.

¹⁹ By wisdom the LORD founded the earth;
   by understanding he created the heavens.
²⁰ By his knowledge the deep fountains of the earth
      burst forth,
   and the dew settles beneath the night sky.

²¹ My child, don't lose sight of common sense and
      discernment.
   Hang on to them,

²² for they will refresh your soul.
>They are like jewels on a necklace.
²³ They keep you safe on your way,
>and your feet will not stumble.
²⁴ You can go to bed without fear;
>you will lie down and sleep soundly.
²⁵ You need not be afraid of sudden disaster
>or the destruction that comes upon the wicked,
²⁶ for the LORD is your security.
>He will keep your foot from being caught in
>a trap.

²⁷ Do not withhold good from those who deserve it
>when it's in your power to help them.
²⁸ If you can help your neighbor now, don't say,
>"Come back tomorrow, and then I'll help you."

²⁹ Don't plot harm against your neighbor,
>for those who live nearby trust you.
³⁰ Don't pick a fight without reason,
>when no one has done you harm.

³¹ Don't envy violent people
>or copy their ways.
³² Such wicked people are detestable to the LORD,
>but he offers his friendship to the godly.

³³ The LORD curses the house of the wicked,
   but he blesses the home of the upright.

³⁴ The LORD mocks the mockers
   but is gracious to the humble.

³⁵ The wise inherit honor,
   but fools are put to shame!

DAY FOUR

🔥 PSALM 16
A psalm of David.

¹ Keep me safe, O God,
  for I have come to you for refuge.

² I said to the LORD, "You are my Master!
  Every good thing I have comes from you."
³ The godly people in the land
  are my true heroes!
  I take pleasure in them!
⁴ Troubles multiply for those who chase after
      other gods.
  I will not take part in their sacrifices of blood
  or even speak the names of their gods.

⁵ LORD, you alone are my inheritance, my cup
      of blessing.
  You guard all that is mine.
⁶ The land you have given me is a pleasant land.
  What a wonderful inheritance!

⁷ I will bless the LORD who guides me;
  even at night my heart instructs me.

⁸ I know the LORD is always with me.
  I will not be shaken, for he is right beside me.

⁹ No wonder my heart is glad, and I rejoice.
  My body rests in safety.
¹⁰ For you will not leave my soul among the dead
  or allow your holy one to rot in the grave.
¹¹ You will show me the way of life,
  granting me the joy of your presence
  and the pleasures of living with you forever.

🔥 PSALM 17

A prayer of David.

¹ O LORD, hear my plea for justice.
  Listen to my cry for help.
Pay attention to my prayer,
  for it comes from honest lips.
² Declare me innocent,
  for you see those who do right.

³ You have tested my thoughts and examined my
  heart in the night.
  You have scrutinized me and found nothing
  wrong.
  I am determined not to sin in what I say.

⁴ I have followed your commands,
   which keep me from following cruel and
      evil people.
⁵ My steps have stayed on your path;
   I have not wavered from following you.

⁶ I am praying to you because I know you will
      answer, O God.
   Bend down and listen as I pray.
⁷ Show me your unfailing love in wonderful ways.
   By your mighty power you rescue
      those who seek refuge from their enemies.
⁸ Guard me as you would guard your own eyes.
   Hide me in the shadow of your wings.
⁹ Protect me from wicked people who attack me,
   from murderous enemies who surround me.
¹⁰ They are without pity.
   Listen to their boasting!
¹¹ They track me down and surround me,
   watching for the chance to throw me to the
      ground.
¹² They are like hungry lions, eager to tear me apart—
   like young lions hiding in ambush.

¹³ Arise, O LORD!

Stand against them, and bring them to their knees!

Rescue me from the wicked with your sword!

¹⁴ By the power of your hand, O Lord,

destroy those who look to this world for their

reward.

But satisfy the hunger of your treasured ones.

May their children have plenty,

leaving an inheritance for their descendants.

¹⁵ Because I am righteous, I will see you.

When I awake, I will see you face to face and

be satisfied.

🌿 PSALM 18

For the choir director: A psalm of David, the servant of the LORD. He sang this song to the LORD on the day the LORD rescued him from all his enemies and from Saul. He sang:

¹ I love you, Lord;

you are my strength.

² The Lord is my rock, my fortress, and my savior;

my God is my rock, in whom I find protection.

He is my shield, the power that saves me,

and my place of safety.

³ I called on the Lord, who is worthy of praise,

and he saved me from my enemies.

⁴ The ropes of death entangled me;
    floods of destruction swept over me.
⁵ The grave wrapped its ropes around me;
    death laid a trap in my path.
⁶ But in my distress I cried out to the LORD;
    yes, I prayed to my God for help.
  He heard me from his sanctuary;
    my cry to him reached his ears.

⁷ Then the earth quaked and trembled.
    The foundations of the mountains shook;
    they quaked because of his anger.
⁸ Smoke poured from his nostrils;
    fierce flames leaped from his mouth.
    Glowing coals blazed forth from him.
⁹ He opened the heavens and came down;
    dark storm clouds were beneath his feet.
¹⁰ Mounted on a mighty angelic being, he flew,
    soaring on the wings of the wind.
¹¹ He shrouded himself in darkness,
    veiling his approach with dark rain clouds.
¹² Thick clouds shielded the brightness
        around him
    and rained down hail and burning coals.
¹³ The LORD thundered from heaven;

the voice of the Most High resounded
amid the hail and burning coals.
14 He shot his arrows and scattered his enemies;
great bolts of lightning flashed, and they were
confused.
15 Then at your command, O LORD,
at the blast of your breath,
the bottom of the sea could be seen,
and the foundations of the earth were
laid bare.

16 He reached down from heaven and rescued me;
he drew me out of deep waters.
17 He rescued me from my powerful enemies,
from those who hated me and were too strong
for me.
18 They attacked me at a moment when I was in
distress,
but the LORD supported me.
19 He led me to a place of safety;
he rescued me because he delights in me.
20 The LORD rewarded me for doing right;
he restored me because of my innocence.
21 For I have kept the ways of the LORD;
I have not turned from my God to follow evil.

²² I have followed all his regulations;
    I have never abandoned his decrees.
²³ I am blameless before God;
    I have kept myself from sin.
²⁴ The LORD rewarded me for doing right.
    He has seen my innocence.

²⁵ To the faithful you show yourself faithful;
    to those with integrity you show integrity.
²⁶ To the pure you show yourself pure,
    but to the crooked you show yourself shrewd.
²⁷ You rescue the humble,
    but you humiliate the proud.
²⁸ You light a lamp for me.
    The LORD, my God, lights up my darkness.
²⁹ In your strength I can crush an army;
    with my God I can scale any wall.

³⁰ God's way is perfect.
    All the LORD's promises prove true.
    He is a shield for all who look to him for
        protection.
³¹ For who is God except the LORD?
    Who but our God is a solid rock?
³² God arms me with strength,
    and he makes my way perfect.

³³ He makes me as surefooted as a deer,
enabling me to stand on mountain heights.
³⁴ He trains my hands for battle;
he strengthens my arm to draw a bronze bow.
³⁵ You have given me your shield of victory.
Your right hand supports me;
your help has made me great.
³⁶ You have made a wide path for my feet
to keep them from slipping.

³⁷ I chased my enemies and caught them;
I did not stop until they were conquered.
³⁸ I struck them down so they could not get up;
they fell beneath my feet.
³⁹ You have armed me with strength for the battle;
you have subdued my enemies under my feet.
⁴⁰ You placed my foot on their necks.
I have destroyed all who hated me.
⁴¹ They called for help, but no one came to their
rescue.
They even cried to the LORD, but he refused
to answer.
⁴² I ground them as fine as dust in the wind.
I swept them into the gutter like dirt.
⁴³ You gave me victory over my accusers.

You appointed me ruler over nations;
people I don't even know now serve me.
⁴⁴ As soon as they hear of me, they submit;
foreign nations cringe before me.
⁴⁵ They all lose their courage
and come trembling from their strongholds.

⁴⁶ The LORD lives! Praise to my Rock!
May the God of my salvation be exalted!
⁴⁷ He is the God who pays back those who harm me;
he subdues the nations under me
⁴⁸ and rescues me from my enemies.
You hold me safe beyond the reach of my enemies;
you save me from violent opponents.
⁴⁹ For this, O LORD, I will praise you among the
nations;
I will sing praises to your name.
⁵⁰ You give great victories to your king;
you show unfailing love to your anointed,
to David and all his descendants forever.

 **PSALM 19**
For the choir director: A psalm of David.

¹ The heavens proclaim the glory of God.
The skies display his craftsmanship.

² Day after day they continue to speak;
   night after night they make him known.
³ They speak without a sound or word;
   their voice is never heard.
⁴ Yet their message has gone throughout the earth,
   and their words to all the world.

God has made a home in the heavens for the sun.
⁵ It bursts forth like a radiant bridegroom after his
      wedding.
   It rejoices like a great athlete eager to run the race.
⁶ The sun rises at one end of the heavens
   and follows its course to the other end.
   Nothing can hide from its heat.

⁷ The instructions of the LORD are perfect,
   reviving the soul.
The decrees of the LORD are trustworthy,
   making wise the simple.
⁸ The commandments of the LORD are right,
   bringing joy to the heart.
The commands of the LORD are clear,
   giving insight for living.
⁹ Reverence for the LORD is pure,
   lasting forever.

The laws of the LORD are true;
  each one is fair.
¹⁰ They are more desirable than gold,
  even the finest gold.
 They are sweeter than honey,
  even honey dripping from the comb.
¹¹ They are a warning to your servant,
  a great reward for those who obey them.

¹² How can I know all the sins lurking in my heart?
  Cleanse me from these hidden faults.
¹³ Keep your servant from deliberate sins!
  Don't let them control me.
 Then I will be free of guilt
  and innocent of great sin.

¹⁴ May the words of my mouth
  and the meditation of my heart
 be pleasing to you,
  O LORD, my rock and my redeemer.

❧ PSALM 20
For the choir director: A psalm of David.

¹ In times of trouble, may the LORD answer your cry.
  May the name of the God of Jacob keep you safe
   from all harm.

² May he send you help from his sanctuary
   and strengthen you from Jerusalem.
³ May he remember all your gifts
   and look favorably on your burnt offerings.

Interlude

⁴ May he grant your heart's desires
   and make all your plans succeed.
⁵ May we shout for joy when we hear of your
      victory
   and raise a victory banner in the name of
      our God.
  May the LORD answer all your prayers.

⁶ Now I know that the LORD rescues his anointed
      king.
   He will answer him from his holy heaven
   and rescue him by his great power.
⁷ Some nations boast of their chariots and horses,
   but we boast in the name of the LORD
      our God.
⁸ Those nations will fall down and collapse,
   but we will rise up and stand firm.

⁹ Give victory to our king, O LORD!
   Answer our cry for help.

✳ PROVERBS 4

1 My children, listen when your father corrects you.
   Pay attention and learn good judgment,
2 for I am giving you good guidance.
   Don't turn away from my instructions.
3 For I, too, was once my father's son,
   tenderly loved as my mother's only child.

4 My father taught me,
   "Take my words to heart.
   Follow my commands, and you will live.
5 Get wisdom; develop good judgment.
   Don't forget my words or turn away from them.
6 Don't turn your back on wisdom, for she will
      protect you.
   Love her, and she will guard you.
7 Getting wisdom is the wisest thing you can do!
   And whatever else you do, develop good judgment.
8 If you prize wisdom, she will make you great.
   Embrace her, and she will honor you.
9 She will place a lovely wreath on your head;
   she will present you with a beautiful crown."

10 My child, listen to me and do as I say,
   and you will have a long, good life.

[11] I will teach you wisdom's ways
     and lead you in straight paths.
[12] When you walk, you won't be held back;
     when you run, you won't stumble.
[13] Take hold of my instructions; don't let them go.
     Guard them, for they are the key to life.

[14] Don't do as the wicked do,
     and don't follow the path of evildoers.
[15] Don't even think about it; don't go that way.
     Turn away and keep moving.
[16] For evil people can't sleep until they've done their
          evil deed for the day.
     They can't rest until they've caused someone
          to stumble.
[17] They eat the food of wickedness
     and drink the wine of violence!

[18] The way of the righteous is like the first gleam
          of dawn,
     which shines ever brighter until the full light of day.
[19] But the way of the wicked is like total darkness.
     They have no idea what they are stumbling over.

[20] My child, pay attention to what I say.
     Listen carefully to my words.

21 Don't lose sight of them.
   Let them penetrate deep into your heart,
22 for they bring life to those who find them,
   and healing to their whole body.

23 Guard your heart above all else,
   for it determines the course of your life.

24 Avoid all perverse talk;
   stay away from corrupt speech.

25 Look straight ahead,
   and fix your eyes on what lies before you.
26 Mark out a straight path for your feet;
   stay on the safe path.
27 Don't get sidetracked;
   keep your feet from following evil.

🕯 PSALM 21

For the choir director: A psalm of David.

¹ How the king rejoices in your strength, O LORD!
    He shouts with joy because you give him victory.
² For you have given him his heart's desire;
    you have withheld nothing he requested.

Interlude

³ You welcomed him back with success and
        prosperity.
    You placed a crown of finest gold on his head.
⁴ He asked you to preserve his life,
    and you granted his request.
    The days of his life stretch on forever.
⁵ Your victory brings him great honor,
    and you have clothed him with splendor and
        majesty.
⁶ You have endowed him with eternal blessings
    and given him the joy of your presence.
⁷ For the king trusts in the LORD.
    The unfailing love of the Most High will keep
        him from stumbling.

⁸ You will capture all your enemies.

Your strong right hand will seize all who hate you.

⁹ You will throw them in a flaming furnace

when you appear.

The LORD will consume them in his anger;

fire will devour them.

¹⁰ You will wipe their children from the face of

the earth;

they will never have descendants.

¹¹ Although they plot against you,

their evil schemes will never succeed.

¹² For they will turn and run

when they see your arrows aimed at them.

¹³ Rise up, O LORD, in all your power.

With music and singing we celebrate your

mighty acts.

🔥 PSALM 22

For the choir director: A psalm of David, to be sung to the tune "Doe of the Dawn."

¹ My God, my God, why have you abandoned me?

Why are you so far away when I groan for help?

² Every day I call to you, my God, but you do not

answer.

Every night I lift my voice, but I find no relief.

3 Yet you are holy,
   enthroned on the praises of Israel.
4 Our ancestors trusted in you,
   and you rescued them.
5 They cried out to you and were saved.
   They trusted in you and were never disgraced.

6 But I am a worm and not a man.
   I am scorned and despised by all!
7 Everyone who sees me mocks me.
   They sneer and shake their heads, saying,
8 "Is this the one who relies on the LORD?
   Then let the LORD save him!
   If the LORD loves him so much,
   let the LORD rescue him!"

9 Yet you brought me safely from my mother's
      womb
   and led me to trust you at my mother's breast.
10 I was thrust into your arms at my birth.
   You have been my God from the moment
      I was born.

11 Do not stay so far from me,
   for trouble is near,
   and no one else can help me.

¹² My enemies surround me like a herd of bulls;
   fierce bulls of Bashan have hemmed me in!
¹³ Like lions they open their jaws against me,
   roaring and tearing into their prey.
¹⁴ My life is poured out like water,
   and all my bones are out of joint.
 My heart is like wax,
   melting within me.
¹⁵ My strength has dried up like sunbaked clay.
   My tongue sticks to the roof of my mouth.
   You have laid me in the dust and left me for dead.
¹⁶ My enemies surround me like a pack of dogs;
   an evil gang closes in on me.
   They have pierced my hands and feet.
¹⁷ I can count all my bones.
   My enemies stare at me and gloat.
¹⁸ They divide my garments among themselves
   and throw dice for my clothing.

¹⁹ O Lord, do not stay far away!
   You are my strength; come quickly to my aid!
²⁰ Save me from the sword;
   spare my precious life from these dogs.
²¹ Snatch me from the lion's jaws
   and from the horns of these wild oxen.

²² I will proclaim your name to my brothers and
      sisters.

   I will praise you among your assembled people.
²³ Praise the LORD, all you who fear him!

   Honor him, all you descendants of Jacob!

   Show him reverence, all you descendants of
      Israel!
²⁴ For he has not ignored or belittled the suffering
      of the needy.

   He has not turned his back on them,

   but has listened to their cries for help.

²⁵ I will praise you in the great assembly.

   I will fulfill my vows in the presence of those
      who worship you.
²⁶ The poor will eat and be satisfied.

   All who seek the LORD will praise him.

   Their hearts will rejoice with everlasting joy.
²⁷ The whole earth will acknowledge the LORD and
      return to him.

   All the families of the nations will bow down
      before him.
²⁸ For royal power belongs to the LORD.

   He rules all the nations.

²⁹ Let the rich of the earth feast and worship.
  Bow before him, all who are mortal,
    all whose lives will end as dust.
³⁰ Our children will also serve him.
  Future generations will hear about the wonders
    of the Lord.
³¹ His righteous acts will be told to those not yet born.
  They will hear about everything he has done.

🔥 PSALM 23

A psalm of David.

¹ The LORD is my shepherd;
  I have all that I need.
² He lets me rest in green meadows;
  he leads me beside peaceful streams.
³   He renews my strength.
 He guides me along right paths,
  bringing honor to his name.
⁴ Even when I walk
  through the darkest valley,
 I will not be afraid,
  for you are close beside me.
 Your rod and your staff
  protect and comfort me.

⁵ You prepare a feast for me
    in the presence of my enemies.
You honor me by anointing my head with oil.
    My cup overflows with blessings.
⁶ Surely your goodness and unfailing love will
      pursue me
    all the days of my life,
and I will live in the house of the Lord
    forever.

❦ PSALM 24

A psalm of David.

¹ The earth is the Lord's, and everything in it.
    The world and all its people belong to him.
² For he laid the earth's foundation on the seas
    and built it on the ocean depths.

³ Who may climb the mountain of the Lord?
    Who may stand in his holy place?
⁴ Only those whose hands and hearts are pure,
    who do not worship idols
    and never tell lies.
⁵ They will receive the Lord's blessing
    and have a right relationship with God their
      savior.

⁶ Such people may seek you
and worship in your presence, O God of Jacob.

Interlude

⁷ Open up, ancient gates!
Open up, ancient doors,
and let the King of glory enter.
⁸ Who is the King of glory?
The LORD, strong and mighty;
the LORD, invincible in battle.
⁹ Open up, ancient gates!
Open up, ancient doors,
and let the King of glory enter.
¹⁰ Who is the King of glory?
The LORD of Heaven's Armies—
he is the King of glory.

Interlude

❧ PSALM 25
A psalm of David.

¹ O LORD, I give my life to you.
²   I trust in you, my God!
Do not let me be disgraced,
or let my enemies rejoice in my defeat.
³ No one who trusts in you will ever be disgraced,
but disgrace comes to those who try to deceive
others.

⁴ Show me the right path, O LORD;
    point out the road for me to follow.
⁵ Lead me by your truth and teach me,
    for you are the God who saves me.
    All day long I put my hope in you.
⁶ Remember, O LORD, your compassion and
        unfailing love,
    which you have shown from long ages past.
⁷ Do not remember the rebellious sins of my youth.
    Remember me in the light of your unfailing love,
    for you are merciful, O LORD.

⁸ The LORD is good and does what is right;
    he shows the proper path to those who
        go astray.
⁹ He leads the humble in doing right,
    teaching them his way.
¹⁰ The LORD leads with unfailing love and
        faithfulness
    all who keep his covenant and obey his demands.

¹¹ For the honor of your name, O LORD,
    forgive my many, many sins.
¹² Who are those who fear the LORD?
    He will show them the path they should choose.

¹³ They will live in prosperity,
   and their children will inherit the land.
¹⁴ The LORD is a friend to those who fear him.
   He teaches them his covenant.
¹⁵ My eyes are always on the LORD,
   for he rescues me from the traps of
      my enemies.

¹⁶ Turn to me and have mercy,
   for I am alone and in deep distress.
¹⁷ My problems go from bad to worse.
   Oh, save me from them all!
¹⁸ Feel my pain and see my trouble.
   Forgive all my sins.
¹⁹ See how many enemies I have
   and how viciously they hate me!
²⁰ Protect me! Rescue my life from them!
   Do not let me be disgraced, for in you I take
      refuge.
²¹ May integrity and honesty protect me,
   for I put my hope in you.

²² O God, ransom Israel
   from all its troubles.

✳ PROVERBS 5

1 My son, pay attention to my wisdom;
   listen carefully to my wise counsel.
2 Then you will show discernment,
   and your lips will express what you've
      learned.
3 For the lips of an immoral woman are as sweet
      as honey,
   and her mouth is smoother than oil.
4 But in the end she is as bitter as poison,
   as dangerous as a double-edged sword.
5 Her feet go down to death;
   her steps lead straight to the grave.
6 For she cares nothing about the path to life.
   She staggers down a crooked trail and doesn't
      realize it.

7 So now, my sons, listen to me.
   Never stray from what I am about to say:
8 Stay away from her!
   Don't go near the door of her house!
9 If you do, you will lose your honor
   and will lose to merciless people all you have
      achieved.

[10] Strangers will consume your wealth,
    and someone else will enjoy the fruit of your
        labor.
[11] In the end you will groan in anguish
    when disease consumes your body.
[12] You will say, "How I hated discipline!
    If only I had not ignored all the warnings!
[13] Oh, why didn't I listen to my teachers?
    Why didn't I pay attention to my instructors?
[14] I have come to the brink of utter ruin,
    and now I must face public disgrace."

[15] Drink water from your own well—
    share your love only with your wife.
[16] Why spill the water of your springs in
        the streets,
    having sex with just anyone?
[17] You should reserve it for yourselves.
    Never share it with strangers.

[18] Let your wife be a fountain of blessing for you.
    Rejoice in the wife of your youth.
[19] She is a loving deer, a graceful doe.
    Let her breasts satisfy you always.
    May you always be captivated by her love.

²⁰ Why be captivated, my son, by an immoral
woman,
or fondle the breasts of a promiscuous woman?

²¹ For the LORD sees clearly what a man does,
examining every path he takes.
²² An evil man is held captive by his own sins;
they are ropes that catch and hold him.
²³ He will die for lack of self-control;
he will be lost because of his great foolishness.

DAY SIX

🔥 PSALM 26

A psalm of David.

¹ Declare me innocent, O LORD,
  for I have acted with integrity;
  I have trusted in the LORD without wavering.
² Put me on trial, LORD, and cross-examine me.
  Test my motives and my heart.
³ For I am always aware of your unfailing love,
  and I have lived according to your truth.
⁴ I do not spend time with liars
  or go along with hypocrites.
⁵ I hate the gatherings of those who do evil,
  and I refuse to join in with the wicked.
⁶ I wash my hands to declare my innocence.
  I come to your altar, O LORD,
⁷ singing a song of thanksgiving
  and telling of all your wonders.
⁸ I love your sanctuary, LORD,
  the place where your glorious presence dwells.

⁹ Don't let me suffer the fate of sinners.
  Don't condemn me along with murderers.

¹⁰ Their hands are dirty with evil schemes,
   and they constantly take bribes.
¹¹ But I am not like that; I live with integrity.
   So redeem me and show me mercy.
¹² Now I stand on solid ground,
   and I will publicly praise the LORD.

🕮 PSALM 27

A psalm of David.

¹ The LORD is my light and my salvation—
   so why should I be afraid?
 The LORD is my fortress, protecting me
    from danger,
   so why should I tremble?
² When evil people come to devour me,
   when my enemies and foes attack me,
   they will stumble and fall.
³ Though a mighty army surrounds me,
   my heart will not be afraid.
 Even if I am attacked,
   I will remain confident.

⁴ The one thing I ask of the LORD—
   the thing I seek most—

is to live in the house of the LORD all the days
of my life,
delighting in the LORD's perfections
and meditating in his Temple.
⁵ For he will conceal me there when troubles come;
he will hide me in his sanctuary.
He will place me out of reach on a high rock.
⁶ Then I will hold my head high
above my enemies who surround me.
At his sanctuary I will offer sacrifices with shouts
of joy,
singing and praising the LORD with music.

⁷ Hear me as I pray, O LORD.
Be merciful and answer me!
⁸ My heart has heard you say, "Come and talk
with me."
And my heart responds, "LORD, I am coming."
⁹ Do not turn your back on me.
Do not reject your servant in anger.
You have always been my helper.
Don't leave me now; don't abandon me,
O God of my salvation!
¹⁰ Even if my father and mother abandon me,
the LORD will hold me close.

11 Teach me how to live, O LORD.
   Lead me along the right path,
      for my enemies are waiting for me.
12 Do not let me fall into their hands.
   For they accuse me of things I've never done;
      with every breath they threaten me with violence.
13 Yet I am confident I will see the LORD's goodness
   while I am here in the land of the living.

14 Wait patiently for the LORD.
   Be brave and courageous.
   Yes, wait patiently for the LORD.

🕊 PSALM 28

A psalm of David.

1 I pray to you, O LORD, my rock.
   Do not turn a deaf ear to me.
For if you are silent,
   I might as well give up and die.
2 Listen to my prayer for mercy
   as I cry out to you for help,
   as I lift my hands toward your holy sanctuary.

3 Do not drag me away with the wicked—
   with those who do evil—

those who speak friendly words to their neighbors
     while planning evil in their hearts.
4 Give them the punishment they so richly deserve!
     Measure it out in proportion to their wickedness.
Pay them back for all their evil deeds!
     Give them a taste of what they have done to
       others.
5 They care nothing for what the LORD has done
     or for what his hands have made.
So he will tear them down,
     and they will never be rebuilt!

6 Praise the LORD!
     For he has heard my cry for mercy.
7 The LORD is my strength and shield.
     I trust him with all my heart.
He helps me, and my heart is filled with joy.
     I burst out in songs of thanksgiving.

8 The LORD gives his people strength.
     He is a safe fortress for his anointed king.
9 Save your people!
     Bless Israel, your special possession.
Lead them like a shepherd,
     and carry them in your arms forever.

 **PSALM 29**

A psalm of David.

¹ Honor the LORD, you heavenly beings;
  honor the LORD for his glory and strength.
² Honor the LORD for the glory of his name.
  Worship the LORD in the splendor of his holiness.

³ The voice of the LORD echoes above the sea.
  The God of glory thunders.
  The LORD thunders over the mighty sea.
⁴ The voice of the LORD is powerful;
  the voice of the LORD is majestic.
⁵ The voice of the LORD splits the mighty cedars;
  the LORD shatters the cedars of Lebanon.
⁶ He makes Lebanon's mountains skip like a calf;
  he makes Mount Hermon leap like a young
    wild ox.
⁷ The voice of the LORD strikes
  with bolts of lightning.
⁸ The voice of the LORD makes the barren wilderness
    quake;
  the LORD shakes the wilderness of Kadesh.
⁹ The voice of the LORD twists mighty oaks
  and strips the forests bare.
  In his Temple everyone shouts, "Glory!"

¹⁰ The LORD rules over the floodwaters.
>   The LORD reigns as king forever.
¹¹ The LORD gives his people strength.
>   The LORD blesses them with peace.

🕯 PSALM 30

A psalm of David. A song for the dedication of the Temple.

¹ I will exalt you, LORD, for you rescued me.
>   You refused to let my enemies triumph
>   over me.
² O LORD my God, I cried to you for help,
>   and you restored my health.
³ You brought me up from the grave, O LORD.
>   You kept me from falling into the pit of death.

⁴ Sing to the LORD, all you godly ones!
>   Praise his holy name.
⁵ For his anger lasts only a moment,
>   but his favor lasts a lifetime!
Weeping may last through the night,
>   but joy comes with the morning.

⁶ When I was prosperous, I said,
>   "Nothing can stop me now!"

⁷ Your favor, O LORD, made me as secure as a
    mountain.
  Then you turned away from me, and I was
    shattered.

⁸ I cried out to you, O LORD.
  I begged the Lord for mercy, saying,
⁹ "What will you gain if I die,
    if I sink into the grave?
  Can my dust praise you?
    Can it tell of your faithfulness?
¹⁰ Hear me, LORD, and have mercy on me.
    Help me, O LORD."

¹¹ You have turned my mourning into joyful dancing.
    You have taken away my clothes of mourning
      and clothed me with joy,
¹² that I might sing praises to you and not be silent.
    O LORD my God, I will give you thanks forever!

✳ PROVERBS 6

¹ My child, if you have put up security for a friend's
    debt
    or agreed to guarantee the debt of a stranger—
² if you have trapped yourself by your agreement

and are caught by what you said—
³ follow my advice and save yourself,
for you have placed yourself at your friend's mercy.
Now swallow your pride;
go and beg to have your name erased.
⁴ Don't put it off; do it now!
Don't rest until you do.
⁵ Save yourself like a gazelle escaping from a hunter,
like a bird fleeing from a net.

⁶ Take a lesson from the ants, you lazybones.
Learn from their ways and become wise!
⁷ Though they have no prince
or governor or ruler to make them work,
⁸ they labor hard all summer,
gathering food for the winter.
⁹ But you, lazybones, how long will you sleep?
When will you wake up?
¹⁰ A little extra sleep, a little more slumber,
a little folding of the hands to rest—
¹¹ then poverty will pounce on you like a bandit;
scarcity will attack you like an armed robber.

¹² What are worthless and wicked people like?
They are constant liars,

13 signaling their deceit with a wink of the eye,
   a nudge of the foot, or the wiggle of fingers.
14 Their perverted hearts plot evil,
   and they constantly stir up trouble.
15 But they will be destroyed suddenly,
   broken in an instant beyond all hope
      of healing.

16 There are six things the LORD hates—
   no, seven things he detests:
17 haughty eyes,
   a lying tongue,
   hands that kill the innocent,
18 a heart that plots evil,
   feet that race to do wrong,
19 a false witness who pours out lies,
   a person who sows discord in a family.

20 My son, obey your father's commands,
   and don't neglect your mother's instruction.
21 Keep their words always in your heart.
   Tie them around your neck.
22 When you walk, their counsel will lead you.
   When you sleep, they will protect you.
   When you wake up, they will advise you.

²³ For their command is a lamp
   and their instruction a light;
 their corrective discipline
   is the way to life.
²⁴ It will keep you from the immoral woman,
   from the smooth tongue of a promiscuous
      woman.
²⁵ Don't lust for her beauty.
   Don't let her coy glances seduce you.
²⁶ For a prostitute will bring you to poverty,
   but sleeping with another man's wife will cost
      you your life.
²⁷ Can a man scoop a flame into his lap
   and not have his clothes catch on fire?
²⁸ Can he walk on hot coals
   and not blister his feet?
²⁹ So it is with the man who sleeps with another
      man's wife.
   He who embraces her will not go unpunished.

³⁰ Excuses might be found for a thief
   who steals because he is starving.
³¹ But if he is caught, he must pay back seven times
      what he stole,
   even if he has to sell everything in his house.

³² But the man who commits adultery is an utter fool,
   for he destroys himself.
³³ He will be wounded and disgraced.
   His shame will never be erased.
³⁴ For the woman's jealous husband will be furious,
   and he will show no mercy when he takes
      revenge.
³⁵ He will accept no compensation,
   nor be satisfied with a payoff of any size.

DAY SEVEN

🕯 PSALM 31

For the choir director: A psalm of David.

¹ O LORD, I have come to you for protection;
    don't let me be disgraced.
    Save me, for you do what is right.
² Turn your ear to listen to me;
    rescue me quickly.
  Be my rock of protection,
    a fortress where I will be safe.
³ You are my rock and my fortress.
    For the honor of your name, lead me out
      of this danger.
⁴ Pull me from the trap my enemies set for me,
    for I find protection in you alone.
⁵ I entrust my spirit into your hand.
    Rescue me, LORD, for you are a faithful God.

⁶ I hate those who worship worthless idols.
    I trust in the LORD.
⁷ I will be glad and rejoice in your unfailing love,
    for you have seen my troubles,
    and you care about the anguish of my soul.

⁸ You have not handed me over to my enemies
    but have set me in a safe place.

⁹ Have mercy on me, LORD, for I am in distress.
    Tears blur my eyes.
    My body and soul are withering away.
¹⁰ I am dying from grief;
    my years are shortened by sadness.
  Sin has drained my strength;
    I am wasting away from within.
¹¹ I am scorned by all my enemies
    and despised by my neighbors—
    even my friends are afraid to come
        near me.
  When they see me on the street,
    they run the other way.
¹² I am ignored as if I were dead,
    as if I were a broken pot.
¹³ I have heard the many rumors about me,
    and I am surrounded by terror.
  My enemies conspire against me,
    plotting to take my life.

¹⁴ But I am trusting you, O LORD,
    saying, "You are my God!"

15 My future is in your hands.
  Rescue me from those who hunt me down
    relentlessly.
16 Let your favor shine on your servant.
  In your unfailing love, rescue me.
17 Don't let me be disgraced, O Lord,
  for I call out to you for help.
Let the wicked be disgraced;
  let them lie silent in the grave.
18 Silence their lying lips—
  those proud and arrogant lips that accuse the godly.

19 How great is the goodness
  you have stored up for those who fear you.
You lavish it on those who come to you for
    protection,
  blessing them before the watching world.
20 You hide them in the shelter of your presence,
  safe from those who conspire against them.
You shelter them in your presence,
  far from accusing tongues.

21 Praise the Lord,
  for he has shown me the wonders of his
    unfailing love.

He kept me safe when my city was under
  attack.
²² In panic I cried out,
    "I am cut off from the LORD!"
  But you heard my cry for mercy
    and answered my call for help.

²³ Love the LORD, all you godly ones!
    For the LORD protects those who are loyal to him,
    but he harshly punishes the arrogant.
²⁴ So be strong and courageous,
    all you who put your hope in the LORD!

❧ PSALM 32

A psalm of David.

¹ Oh, what joy for those
    whose disobedience is forgiven,
    whose sin is put out of sight!
² Yes, what joy for those
    whose record the LORD has cleared of guilt,
    whose lives are lived in complete honesty!
³ When I refused to confess my sin,
    my body wasted away,
    and I groaned all day long.

[4] Day and night your hand of discipline was heavy
     on me.
  My strength evaporated like water in the
     summer heat.   *Interlude*

[5] Finally, I confessed all my sins to you
     and stopped trying to hide my guilt.
  I said to myself, "I will confess my rebellion to the
     LORD."
     And you forgave me! All my guilt is gone.
                                               Interlude

[6] Therefore, let all the godly pray to you while there
     is still time,
  that they may not drown in the floodwaters
     of judgment.
[7] For you are my hiding place;
     you protect me from trouble.
  You surround me with songs of victory. *Interlude*

[8] The LORD says, "I will guide you along the best
     pathway for your life.
  I will advise you and watch over you.
[9] Do not be like a senseless horse or mule
     that needs a bit and bridle to keep it under
     control."

¹⁰ Many sorrows come to the wicked,
  but unfailing love surrounds those who trust
   the LORD.
¹¹ So rejoice in the LORD and be glad, all you who
  obey him!
  Shout for joy, all you whose hearts are pure!

❧ PSALM 33

¹ Let the godly sing for joy to the LORD;
  it is fitting for the pure to praise him.
² Praise the LORD with melodies on the lyre;
  make music for him on the ten-stringed harp.
³ Sing a new song of praise to him;
  play skillfully on the harp, and sing with joy.
⁴ For the word of the LORD holds true,
  and we can trust everything he does.
⁵ He loves whatever is just and good;
  the unfailing love of the LORD fills the earth.

⁶ The LORD merely spoke,
  and the heavens were created.
 He breathed the word,
  and all the stars were born.
⁷ He assigned the sea its boundaries
  and locked the oceans in vast reservoirs.

⁸ Let the whole world fear the LORD,
   and let everyone stand in awe of him.
⁹ For when he spoke, the world began!
   It appeared at his command.

¹⁰ The LORD frustrates the plans of the nations
   and thwarts all their schemes.
¹¹ But the LORD's plans stand firm forever;
   his intentions can never be shaken.

¹² What joy for the nation whose God is the LORD,
   whose people he has chosen as his inheritance.

¹³ The LORD looks down from heaven
   and sees the whole human race.
¹⁴ From his throne he observes
   all who live on the earth.
¹⁵ He made their hearts,
   so he understands everything they do.
¹⁶ The best-equipped army cannot save a king,
   nor is great strength enough to save a warrior.
¹⁷ Don't count on your warhorse to give you
      victory—
   for all its strength, it cannot save you.

¹⁸ But the LORD watches over those who fear him,
   those who rely on his unfailing love.

¹⁹ He rescues them from death
>> and keeps them alive in times of famine.

²⁰ We put our hope in the LORD.
>> He is our help and our shield.
²¹ In him our hearts rejoice,
>> for we trust in his holy name.
²² Let your unfailing love surround us, LORD,
>> for our hope is in you alone.

❧ PSALM 34

A psalm of David, regarding the time he pretended to be insane in front of Abimelech, who sent him away.

¹ I will praise the LORD at all times.
>> I will constantly speak his praises.
² I will boast only in the LORD;
>> let all who are helpless take heart.
³ Come, let us tell of the LORD's greatness;
>> let us exalt his name together.

⁴ I prayed to the LORD, and he answered me.
>> He freed me from all my fears.
⁵ Those who look to him for help will be radiant
>>> with joy;
>> no shadow of shame will darken their faces.

6 In my desperation I prayed, and the LORD
    listened;
    he saved me from all my troubles.
7 For the angel of the LORD is a guard;
    he surrounds and defends all who fear him.

8 Taste and see that the LORD is good.
    Oh, the joys of those who take refuge in him!
9 Fear the LORD, you his godly people,
    for those who fear him will have all they need.
10 Even strong young lions sometimes go hungry,
    but those who trust in the LORD will lack no
    good thing.

11 Come, my children, and listen to me,
    and I will teach you to fear the LORD.
12 Does anyone want to live a life
    that is long and prosperous?
13 Then keep your tongue from speaking evil
    and your lips from telling lies!
14 Turn away from evil and do good.
    Search for peace, and work to maintain it.

15 The eyes of the LORD watch over those who
    do right;
    his ears are open to their cries for help.

[16] But the LORD turns his face against those who
do evil;
he will erase their memory from the earth.
[17] The LORD hears his people when they call to
him for help.
He rescues them from all their troubles.
[18] The LORD is close to the brokenhearted;
he rescues those whose spirits are crushed.

[19] The righteous person faces many troubles,
but the LORD comes to the rescue each time.
[20] For the LORD protects the bones of the righteous;
not one of them is broken!

[21] Calamity will surely destroy the wicked,
and those who hate the righteous will be
punished.
[22] But the LORD will redeem those who serve him.
No one who takes refuge in him will be
condemned.

❧ PSALM 35

A psalm of David.

[1] O LORD, oppose those who oppose me.
Fight those who fight against me.

² Put on your armor, and take up your shield.
   Prepare for battle, and come to my aid.
³ Lift up your spear and javelin
   against those who pursue me.
  Let me hear you say,
   "I will give you victory!"
⁴ Bring shame and disgrace on those trying to kill me;
   turn them back and humiliate those who want
      to harm me.
⁵ Blow them away like chaff in the wind—
   a wind sent by the angel of the LORD.
⁶ Make their path dark and slippery,
   with the angel of the LORD pursuing them.
⁷ I did them no wrong, but they laid a trap for me.
   I did them no wrong, but they dug a pit to
      catch me.
⁸ So let sudden ruin come upon them!
   Let them be caught in the trap they set for me!
   Let them be destroyed in the pit they dug for me.

⁹ Then I will rejoice in the LORD.
   I will be glad because he rescues me.
¹⁰ With every bone in my body I will praise him:
   "LORD, who can compare with you?
  Who else rescues the helpless from the strong?

Who else protects the helpless and poor from
those who rob them?"

¹¹ Malicious witnesses testify against me.
They accuse me of crimes I know nothing about.
¹² They repay me evil for good.
I am sick with despair.
¹³ Yet when they were ill, I grieved for them.
I denied myself by fasting for them,
but my prayers returned unanswered.
¹⁴ I was sad, as though they were my friends or family,
as if I were grieving for my own mother.
¹⁵ But they are glad now that I am in trouble;
they gleefully join together against me.
I am attacked by people I don't even know;
they slander me constantly.
¹⁶ They mock me and call me names;
they snarl at me.

¹⁷ How long, O Lord, will you look on and do
nothing?
Rescue me from their fierce attacks.
Protect my life from these lions!
¹⁸ Then I will thank you in front of the great assembly.
I will praise you before all the people.

¹⁹ Don't let my treacherous enemies rejoice over my
    defeat.
    Don't let those who hate me without cause gloat
      over my sorrow.
²⁰ They don't talk of peace;
    they plot against innocent people who mind
      their own business.
²¹ They shout, "Aha! Aha!
    With our own eyes we saw him do it!"

²² O LORD, you know all about this.
    Do not stay silent.
    Do not abandon me now, O Lord.
²³ Wake up! Rise to my defense!
    Take up my case, my God and my Lord.
²⁴ Declare me not guilty, O LORD my God, for you
    give justice.
    Don't let my enemies laugh about me in my
      troubles.
²⁵ Don't let them say, "Look, we got what we
    wanted!
    Now we will eat him alive!"

²⁶ May those who rejoice at my troubles
    be humiliated and disgraced.

May those who triumph over me
  be covered with shame and dishonor.
²⁷ But give great joy to those who came to my defense.
  Let them continually say, "Great is the LORD,
  who delights in blessing his servant with peace!"
²⁸ Then I will proclaim your justice,
  and I will praise you all day long.

✳ PROVERBS 7

¹ Follow my advice, my son;
  always treasure my commands.
² Obey my commands and live!
  Guard my instructions as you guard your own eyes.
³ Tie them on your fingers as a reminder.
  Write them deep within your heart.

⁴ Love wisdom like a sister;
  make insight a beloved member of your family.
⁵ Let them protect you from an affair with an
    immoral woman,
  from listening to the flattery of a promiscuous
    woman.

⁶ While I was at the window of my house,
  looking through the curtain,

7 I saw some naive young men,
  and one in particular who lacked common
    sense.
8 He was crossing the street near the house of an
    immoral woman,
  strolling down the path by her house.
9 It was at twilight, in the evening,
  as deep darkness fell.
10 The woman approached him,
  seductively dressed and sly of heart.
11 She was the brash, rebellious type,
  never content to stay at home.
12 She is often in the streets and markets,
  soliciting at every corner.
13 She threw her arms around him and kissed him,
  and with a brazen look she said,
14 "I've just made my peace offerings
  and fulfilled my vows.
15 You're the one I was looking for!
  I came out to find you, and here you are!
16 My bed is spread with beautiful blankets,
  with colored sheets of Egyptian linen.
17 I've perfumed my bed
  with myrrh, aloes, and cinnamon.

¹⁸ Come, let's drink our fill of love until morning.
    Let's enjoy each other's caresses,
¹⁹ for my husband is not home.
    He's away on a long trip.
²⁰ He has taken a wallet full of money with him
    and won't return until later this month."

²¹ So she seduced him with her pretty speech
    and enticed him with her flattery.
²² He followed her at once,
    like an ox going to the slaughter.
  He was like a stag caught in a trap,
²³   awaiting the arrow that would pierce its heart.
  He was like a bird flying into a snare,
    little knowing it would cost him his life.

²⁴ So listen to me, my sons,
    and pay attention to my words.
²⁵ Don't let your hearts stray away toward her.
    Don't wander down her wayward path.
²⁶ For she has been the ruin of many;
    many men have been her victims.
²⁷ Her house is the road to the grave.
    Her bedroom is the den of death.

DAY EIGHT

🔥 PSALM 36

For the choir director: A psalm of David, the servant of the LORD.

¹ Sin whispers to the wicked, deep within their hearts.
　　They have no fear of God at all.
² In their blind conceit,
　　they cannot see how wicked they really are.
³ Everything they say is crooked and deceitful.
　　They refuse to act wisely or do good.
⁴ They lie awake at night, hatching sinful plots.
　　Their actions are never good.
　　They make no attempt to turn from evil.

⁵ Your unfailing love, O LORD, is as vast as the heavens;
　　your faithfulness reaches beyond the clouds.
⁶ Your righteousness is like the mighty mountains,
　　your justice like the ocean depths.
　You care for people and animals alike, O LORD.
⁷ 　How precious is your unfailing love, O God!
　All humanity finds shelter
　　in the shadow of your wings.
⁸ You feed them from the abundance of your own
　　　　house,
　　letting them drink from your river of delights.

⁹ For you are the fountain of life,
   the light by which we see.

¹⁰ Pour out your unfailing love on those who
      love you;
   give justice to those with honest hearts.
¹¹ Don't let the proud trample me
   or the wicked push me around.
¹² Look! Those who do evil have fallen!
   They are thrown down, never to rise again.

🔥 PSALM 37

A psalm of David.

¹ Don't worry about the wicked
   or envy those who do wrong.
² For like grass, they soon fade away.
   Like spring flowers, they soon wither.

³ Trust in the LORD and do good.
   Then you will live safely in the land and prosper.
⁴ Take delight in the LORD,
   and he will give you your heart's desires.

⁵ Commit everything you do to the LORD.
   Trust him, and he will help you.
⁶ He will make your innocence radiate like the dawn,

and the justice of your cause will shine like
the noonday sun.

⁷ Be still in the presence of the LORD,
and wait patiently for him to act.
Don't worry about evil people who prosper
or fret about their wicked schemes.

⁸ Stop being angry!
Turn from your rage!
Do not lose your temper—
it only leads to harm.
⁹ For the wicked will be destroyed,
but those who trust in the LORD will possess
the land.

¹⁰ Soon the wicked will disappear.
Though you look for them, they will be gone.
¹¹ The lowly will possess the land
and will live in peace and prosperity.

¹² The wicked plot against the godly;
they snarl at them in defiance.
¹³ But the Lord just laughs,
for he sees their day of judgment coming.

¹⁴ The wicked draw their swords
and string their bows

to kill the poor and the oppressed,
   to slaughter those who do right.
¹⁵ But their swords will stab their own hearts,
   and their bows will be broken.

¹⁶ It is better to be godly and have little
   than to be evil and rich.
¹⁷ For the strength of the wicked will be shattered,
   but the LORD takes care of the godly.

¹⁸ Day by day the LORD takes care of the innocent,
   and they will receive an inheritance that lasts
      forever.
¹⁹ They will not be disgraced in hard times;
   even in famine they will have more than enough.

²⁰ But the wicked will die.
   The LORD's enemies are like flowers in a field—
   they will disappear like smoke.

²¹ The wicked borrow and never repay,
   but the godly are generous givers.
²² Those the LORD blesses will possess the land,
   but those he curses will die.

²³ The LORD directs the steps of the godly.
   He delights in every detail of their lives.

²⁴ Though they stumble, they will never fall,
for the LORD holds them by the hand.

²⁵ Once I was young, and now I am old.
Yet I have never seen the godly abandoned
or their children begging for bread.
²⁶ The godly always give generous loans to
others,
and their children are a blessing.

²⁷ Turn from evil and do good,
and you will live in the land forever.
²⁸ For the LORD loves justice,
and he will never abandon the godly.

He will keep them safe forever,
but the children of the wicked will die.
²⁹ The godly will possess the land
and will live there forever.

³⁰ The godly offer good counsel;
they teach right from wrong.
³¹ They have made God's law their own,
so they will never slip from his path.

³² The wicked wait in ambush for the godly,
looking for an excuse to kill them.

³³ But the Lord will not let the wicked succeed
    or let the godly be condemned when they are put
        on trial.

³⁴ Put your hope in the Lord.
    Travel steadily along his path.
  He will honor you by giving you the land.
    You will see the wicked destroyed.

³⁵ I have seen wicked and ruthless people
    flourishing like a tree in its native soil.
³⁶ But when I looked again, they were gone!
    Though I searched for them, I could not find
        them!

³⁷ Look at those who are honest and good,
    for a wonderful future awaits those who love
        peace.
³⁸ But the rebellious will be destroyed;
    they have no future.

³⁹ The Lord rescues the godly;
    he is their fortress in times of trouble.
⁴⁰ The Lord helps them,
    rescuing them from the wicked.
  He saves them,
    and they find shelter in him.

🌱 PSALM 38

A psalm of David, asking God to remember him.

¹ O LORD, don't rebuke me in your anger
  or discipline me in your rage!
² Your arrows have struck deep,
  and your blows are crushing me.
³ Because of your anger, my whole body is sick;
  my health is broken because of my sins.
⁴ My guilt overwhelms me—
  it is a burden too heavy to bear.
⁵ My wounds fester and stink
  because of my foolish sins.
⁶ I am bent over and racked with pain.
  All day long I walk around filled with grief.
⁷ A raging fever burns within me,
  and my health is broken.
⁸ I am exhausted and completely crushed.
  My groans come from an anguished heart.

⁹ You know what I long for, Lord;
  you hear my every sigh.
¹⁰ My heart beats wildly, my strength fails,
  and I am going blind.
¹¹ My loved ones and friends stay away, fearing my
     disease.

Even my own family stands at a distance.

¹² Meanwhile, my enemies lay traps to kill me.
Those who wish me harm make plans to ruin me.
All day long they plan their treachery.

¹³ But I am deaf to all their threats.
I am silent before them as one who cannot speak.

¹⁴ I choose to hear nothing,
and I make no reply.

¹⁵ For I am waiting for you, O Lord.
You must answer for me, O Lord my God.

¹⁶ I prayed, "Don't let my enemies gloat over me
or rejoice at my downfall."

¹⁷ I am on the verge of collapse,
facing constant pain.

¹⁸ But I confess my sins;
I am deeply sorry for what I have done.

¹⁹ I have many aggressive enemies;
they hate me without reason.

²⁰ They repay me evil for good
and oppose me for pursuing good.

²¹ Do not abandon me, O Lord.
Do not stand at a distance, my God.

²² Come quickly to help me,
O Lord my savior.

❧ PSALM 39

For Jeduthun, the choir director: A psalm of David.

¹ I said to myself, "I will watch what I do
    and not sin in what I say.
 I will hold my tongue
    when the ungodly are around me."
² But as I stood there in silence—
    not even speaking of good things—
    the turmoil within me grew worse.
³ The more I thought about it,
    the hotter I got,
    igniting a fire of words:
⁴ "LORD, remind me how brief my time on earth
    will be.
 Remind me that my days are numbered—
    how fleeting my life is.
⁵ You have made my life no longer than the width
    of my hand.
 My entire lifetime is just a moment to you;
    at best, each of us is but a breath."   *Interlude*

⁶ We are merely moving shadows,
    and all our busy rushing ends in nothing.
 We heap up wealth,
    not knowing who will spend it.

⁷ And so, Lord, where do I put my hope?

    My only hope is in you.

⁸ Rescue me from my rebellion.

    Do not let fools mock me.

⁹ I am silent before you; I won't say a word,

    for my punishment is from you.

¹⁰ But please stop striking me!

    I am exhausted by the blows from your hand.

¹¹ When you discipline us for our sins,

    you consume like a moth what is precious to us.

    Each of us is but a breath. *Interlude*

¹² Hear my prayer, O LORD!

    Listen to my cries for help!

    Don't ignore my tears.

  For I am your guest—

    a traveler passing through,

    as my ancestors were before me.

¹³ Leave me alone so I can smile again

    before I am gone and exist no more.

🔥 PSALM 40

For the choir director: A psalm of David.

¹ I waited patiently for the LORD to help me,

    and he turned to me and heard my cry.

² He lifted me out of the pit of despair,
   out of the mud and the mire.
He set my feet on solid ground
   and steadied me as I walked along.
³ He has given me a new song to sing,
   a hymn of praise to our God.
Many will see what he has done and be amazed.
   They will put their trust in the LORD.

⁴ Oh, the joys of those who trust the LORD,
   who have no confidence in the proud
   or in those who worship idols.
⁵ O LORD my God, you have performed many
      wonders for us.
   Your plans for us are too numerous to list.
   You have no equal.
If I tried to recite all your wonderful deeds,
   I would never come to the end of them.

⁶ You take no delight in sacrifices or offerings.
   Now that you have made me listen, I finally
      understand—
   you don't require burnt offerings or sin offerings.
⁷ Then I said, "Look, I have come.
   As is written about me in the Scriptures:

⁸ I take joy in doing your will, my God,
     for your instructions are written on my heart."

⁹ I have told all your people about your justice.
     I have not been afraid to speak out,
          as you, O Lord, well know.
¹⁰ I have not kept the good news of your justice
          hidden in my heart;
     I have talked about your faithfulness and saving
          power.
I have told everyone in the great assembly
     of your unfailing love and faithfulness.

¹¹ Lord, don't hold back your tender mercies
          from me.
     Let your unfailing love and faithfulness always
          protect me.
¹² For troubles surround me—
     too many to count!
My sins pile up so high
     I can't see my way out.
They outnumber the hairs on my head.
     I have lost all courage.

¹³ Please, Lord, rescue me!
     Come quickly, Lord, and help me.

¹⁴ May those who try to destroy me
    be humiliated and put to shame.
May those who take delight in my trouble
    be turned back in disgrace.
¹⁵ Let them be horrified by their shame,
    for they said, "Aha! We've got him now!"

¹⁶ But may all who search for you
    be filled with joy and gladness in you.
May those who love your salvation
    repeatedly shout, "The LORD is great!"
¹⁷ As for me, since I am poor and needy,
    let the Lord keep me in his thoughts.
You are my helper and my savior.
    O my God, do not delay.

✳ PROVERBS 8

¹ Listen as Wisdom calls out!
    Hear as understanding raises her voice!
² On the hilltop along the road,
    she takes her stand at the crossroads.
³ By the gates at the entrance to the town,
    on the road leading in, she cries aloud,
⁴ "I call to you, to all of you!
    I raise my voice to all people.

5 You simple people, use good judgment.
   You foolish people, show some understanding.
6 Listen to me! For I have important things to tell you.
   Everything I say is right,
7 for I speak the truth
   and detest every kind of deception.
8 My advice is wholesome.
   There is nothing devious or crooked in it.
9 My words are plain to anyone with understanding,
   clear to those with knowledge.
10 Choose my instruction rather than silver,
   and knowledge rather than pure gold.
11 For wisdom is far more valuable than rubies.
   Nothing you desire can compare with it.

12 "I, Wisdom, live together with good judgment.
   I know where to discover knowledge and
      discernment.
13 All who fear the LORD will hate evil.
   Therefore, I hate pride and arrogance,
      corruption and perverse speech.
14 Common sense and success belong to me.
   Insight and strength are mine.
15 Because of me, kings reign,
   and rulers make just decrees.

¹⁶ Rulers lead with my help,
   and nobles make righteous judgments.

¹⁷ "I love all who love me.
   Those who search will surely find me.
¹⁸ I have riches and honor,
   as well as enduring wealth and justice.
¹⁹ My gifts are better than gold, even the purest gold,
   my wages better than sterling silver!
²⁰ I walk in righteousness,
   in paths of justice.
²¹ Those who love me inherit wealth.
   I will fill their treasuries.

²² "The LORD formed me from the beginning,
   before he created anything else.
²³ I was appointed in ages past,
   at the very first, before the earth began.
²⁴ I was born before the oceans were created,
   before the springs bubbled forth their waters.
²⁵ Before the mountains were formed,
   before the hills, I was born—
²⁶ before he had made the earth and fields
   and the first handfuls of soil.
²⁷ I was there when he established the heavens,
   when he drew the horizon on the oceans.

28 I was there when he set the clouds above,
   when he established springs deep in the earth.
29 I was there when he set the limits of the seas,
   so they would not spread beyond their
      boundaries.
   And when he marked off the earth's foundations,
30   I was the architect at his side.
   I was his constant delight,
      rejoicing always in his presence.
31 And how happy I was with the world he created;
   how I rejoiced with the human family!

32 "And so, my children, listen to me,
   for all who follow my ways are joyful.
33 Listen to my instruction and be wise.
   Don't ignore it.
34 Joyful are those who listen to me,
   watching for me daily at my gates,
   waiting for me outside my home!
35 For whoever finds me finds life
   and receives favor from the LORD.
36 But those who miss me injure themselves.
   All who hate me love death."

DAY NINE

🔥 PSALM 41

For the choir director: A psalm of David.

¹ Oh, the joys of those who are kind to the poor!
   The LORD rescues them when they are in trouble.
² The LORD protects them
   and keeps them alive.
  He gives them prosperity in the land
   and rescues them from their enemies.
³ The LORD nurses them when they are sick
   and restores them to health.

⁴ "O LORD," I prayed, "have mercy on me.
   Heal me, for I have sinned against you."
⁵ But my enemies say nothing but evil about me.
   "How soon will he die and be forgotten?"
      they ask.
⁶ They visit me as if they were my friends,
   but all the while they gather gossip,
   and when they leave, they spread it
      everywhere.
⁷ All who hate me whisper about me,
   imagining the worst.

8 "He has some fatal disease," they say.
"He will never get out of that bed!"
9 Even my best friend, the one I trusted completely,
the one who shared my food, has turned
against me.

10 LORD, have mercy on me.
Make me well again, so I can pay them back!
11 I know you are pleased with me,
for you have not let my enemies triumph
over me.
12 You have preserved my life because I am innocent;
you have brought me into your presence forever.

13 Praise the LORD, the God of Israel,
who lives from everlasting to everlasting.
Amen and amen!

BOOK TWO (PSALMS 42–72)

🔥 **PSALM 42**
For the choir director: A psalm of the descendants of Korah.

1 As the deer longs for streams of water,
so I long for you, O God.
2 I thirst for God, the living God.
When can I go and stand before him?

[3] Day and night I have only tears for food,
  while my enemies continually taunt me, saying,
  "Where is this God of yours?"

[4] My heart is breaking
  as I remember how it used to be:
I walked among the crowds of worshipers,
  leading a great procession to the house of God,
singing for joy and giving thanks
  amid the sound of a great celebration!

[5] Why am I discouraged?
  Why is my heart so sad?
I will put my hope in God!
  I will praise him again—
  my Savior and [6]my God!

Now I am deeply discouraged,
  but I will remember you—
even from distant Mount Hermon, the source
    of the Jordan,
  from the land of Mount Mizar.
[7] I hear the tumult of the raging seas
  as your waves and surging tides sweep over me.
[8] But each day the LORD pours his unfailing love
    upon me,

and through each night I sing his songs,
 praying to God who gives me life.

9 "O God my rock," I cry,
 "Why have you forgotten me?
Why must I wander around in grief,
 oppressed by my enemies?"
10 Their taunts break my bones.
 They scoff, "Where is this God of yours?"

11 Why am I discouraged?
 Why is my heart so sad?
I will put my hope in God!
 I will praise him again—
 my Savior and my God!

❦ PSALM 43

1 Declare me innocent, O God!
 Defend me against these ungodly people.
 Rescue me from these unjust liars.
2 For you are God, my only safe haven.
 Why have you tossed me aside?
Why must I wander around in grief,
 oppressed by my enemies?

³ Send out your light and your truth;
   let them guide me.
Let them lead me to your holy mountain,
   to the place where you live.
⁴ There I will go to the altar of God,
   to God—the source of all my joy.
I will praise you with my harp,
   O God, my God!

⁵ Why am I discouraged?
   Why is my heart so sad?
I will put my hope in God!
   I will praise him again—
   my Savior and my God!

❦ PSALM 44

For the choir director: A psalm of the descendants of Korah.

¹ O God, we have heard it with our own ears—
   our ancestors have told us
of all you did in their day,
   in days long ago:
² You drove out the pagan nations by your power
   and gave all the land to our ancestors.
You crushed their enemies
   and set our ancestors free.

³ They did not conquer the land with their swords;
   it was not their own strong arm that gave
      them victory.
  It was your right hand and strong arm
     and the blinding light from your face that
        helped them,
     for you loved them.

⁴ You are my King and my God.
     You command victories for Israel.
⁵ Only by your power can we push back our enemies;
     only in your name can we trample our foes.
⁶ I do not trust in my bow;
     I do not count on my sword to save me.
⁷ You are the one who gives us victory over our
        enemies;
     you disgrace those who hate us.
⁸ O God, we give glory to you all day long
     and constantly praise your name.   *Interlude*

⁹ But now you have tossed us aside in dishonor.
     You no longer lead our armies to battle.
¹⁰ You make us retreat from our enemies
     and allow those who hate us to plunder
        our land.

¹¹ You have butchered us like sheep
    and scattered us among the nations.
¹² You sold your precious people for a pittance,
    making nothing on the sale.
¹³ You let our neighbors mock us.
    We are an object of scorn and derision to
        those around us.
¹⁴ You have made us the butt of their jokes;
    they shake their heads at us in scorn.
¹⁵ We can't escape the constant humiliation;
    shame is written across our faces.
¹⁶ All we hear are the taunts of our mockers.
    All we see are our vengeful enemies.

¹⁷ All this has happened though we have not
      forgotten you.
    We have not violated your covenant.
¹⁸ Our hearts have not deserted you.
    We have not strayed from your path.
¹⁹ Yet you have crushed us in the jackal's desert home.
    You have covered us with darkness and death.
²⁰ If we had forgotten the name of our God
    or spread our hands in prayer to foreign gods,
²¹ God would surely have known it,
    for he knows the secrets of every heart.

²² But for your sake we are killed every day;
   we are being slaughtered like sheep.

²³ Wake up, O Lord! Why do you sleep?
   Get up! Do not reject us forever.
²⁴ Why do you look the other way?
   Why do you ignore our suffering and
      oppression?
²⁵ We collapse in the dust,
   lying face down in the dirt.
²⁶ Rise up! Help us!
   Ransom us because of your unfailing love.

🌿 **PSALM 45**

For the choir director: A love song to be sung to the tune "Lilies."
A psalm of the descendants of Korah.

¹ Beautiful words stir my heart.
   I will recite a lovely poem about the king,
      for my tongue is like the pen of a skillful poet.

² You are the most handsome of all.
   Gracious words stream from your lips.
   God himself has blessed you forever.
³ Put on your sword, O mighty warrior!
   You are so glorious, so majestic!

⁴ In your majesty, ride out to victory,
    defending truth, humility, and justice.
    Go forth to perform awe-inspiring deeds!
⁵ Your arrows are sharp, piercing your enemies'
        hearts.
    The nations fall beneath your feet.

⁶ Your throne, O God, endures forever and ever.
    You rule with a scepter of justice.
⁷ You love justice and hate evil.
    Therefore God, your God, has anointed you,
    pouring out the oil of joy on you more than
        on anyone else.
⁸ Myrrh, aloes, and cassia perfume your robes.
    In ivory palaces the music of strings entertains
        you.
⁹ Kings' daughters are among your noble women.
    At your right side stands the queen,
    wearing jewelry of finest gold from Ophir!

¹⁰ Listen to me, O royal daughter; take to heart
        what I say.
    Forget your people and your family far away.
¹¹ For your royal husband delights in your beauty;
    honor him, for he is your lord.

¹² The princess of Tyre will shower you with gifts.
   The wealthy will beg your favor.
¹³ The bride, a princess, looks glorious
   in her golden gown.
¹⁴ In her beautiful robes, she is led to the king,
   accompanied by her bridesmaids.
¹⁵ What a joyful and enthusiastic procession
   as they enter the king's palace!

¹⁶ Your sons will become kings like their father.
   You will make them rulers over many lands.
¹⁷ I will bring honor to your name in every
      generation.
   Therefore, the nations will praise you forever
      and ever.

✳ PROVERBS 9

¹ Wisdom has built her house;
   she has carved its seven columns.
² She has prepared a great banquet,
   mixed the wines, and set the table.
³ She has sent her servants to invite everyone
      to come.
   She calls out from the heights overlooking
      the city.

⁴ "Come in with me," she urges the simple.
    To those who lack good judgment, she says,
⁵ "Come, eat my food,
    and drink the wine I have mixed.
⁶ Leave your simple ways behind, and begin
        to live;
    learn to use good judgment."

⁷ Anyone who rebukes a mocker will get an insult
        in return.
    Anyone who corrects the wicked will get hurt.
⁸ So don't bother correcting mockers;
    they will only hate you.
  But correct the wise,
    and they will love you.
⁹ Instruct the wise,
    and they will be even wiser.
  Teach the righteous,
    and they will learn even more.

¹⁰ Fear of the LORD is the foundation of wisdom.
    Knowledge of the Holy One results in good
        judgment.

¹¹ Wisdom will multiply your days
    and add years to your life.

¹² If you become wise, you will be the one to benefit.
    If you scorn wisdom, you will be the one to
        suffer.

¹³ The woman named Folly is brash.
    She is ignorant and doesn't know it.
¹⁴ She sits in her doorway
    on the heights overlooking the city.
¹⁵ She calls out to men going by
    who are minding their own business.
¹⁶ "Come in with me," she urges the simple.
    To those who lack good judgment, she says,
¹⁷ "Stolen water is refreshing;
    food eaten in secret tastes the best!"
¹⁸ But little do they know that the dead are there.
    Her guests are in the depths of the grave.

DAY TEN

🔥 PSALM 46

For the choir director: A song of the descendants of Korah, to be sung by soprano voices.

¹ God is our refuge and strength,
   always ready to help in times of trouble.
² So we will not fear when earthquakes come
   and the mountains crumble into the sea.
³ Let the oceans roar and foam.
   Let the mountains tremble as the
      waters surge!   *Interlude*

⁴ A river brings joy to the city of our God,
   the sacred home of the Most High.
⁵ God dwells in that city; it cannot be destroyed.
   From the very break of day, God will
      protect it.
⁶ The nations are in chaos,
   and their kingdoms crumble!
God's voice thunders,
   and the earth melts!
⁷ The LORD of Heaven's Armies is here among us;
   the God of Israel is our fortress.   *Interlude*

⁸ Come, see the glorious works of the LORD:
　　See how he brings destruction upon
　　　the world.
⁹ He causes wars to end throughout the earth.
　　He breaks the bow and snaps the spear;
　　he burns the shields with fire.

¹⁰ "Be still, and know that I am God!
　　I will be honored by every nation.
　　I will be honored throughout the world."

¹¹ The LORD of Heaven's Armies is here among us;
　　the God of Israel is our fortress.　　　*Interlude*

🌱 PSALM 47

For the choir director: A psalm of the descendants of Korah.

¹ Come, everyone! Clap your hands!
　　Shout to God with joyful praise!
² For the LORD Most High is awesome.
　　He is the great King of all the earth.
³ He subdues the nations before us,
　　putting our enemies beneath our feet.
⁴ He chose the Promised Land as our inheritance,
　　the proud possession of Jacob's descendants,
　　　whom he loves.　　　*Interlude*

[5] God has ascended with a mighty shout.
>> The LORD has ascended with trumpets
>> blaring.
[6] Sing praises to God, sing praises;
>> sing praises to our King, sing praises!
[7] For God is the King over all the earth.
>> Praise him with a psalm.
[8] God reigns above the nations,
>> sitting on his holy throne.
[9] The rulers of the world have gathered together
>> with the people of the God of Abraham.
> For all the kings of the earth belong to God.
>> He is highly honored everywhere.

✹ PSALM 48

A song. A psalm of the descendants of Korah.

[1] How great is the LORD,
>> how deserving of praise,
> in the city of our God,
>> which sits on his holy mountain!
[2] It is high and magnificent;
>> the whole earth rejoices to see it!
> Mount Zion, the holy mountain,
>> is the city of the great King!

³ God himself is in Jerusalem's towers,
   revealing himself as its defender.

⁴ The kings of the earth joined forces
   and advanced against the city.
⁵ But when they saw it, they were stunned;
   they were terrified and ran away.
⁶ They were gripped with terror
   and writhed in pain like a woman in labor.
⁷ You destroyed them like the mighty ships of Tarshish
   shattered by a powerful east wind.

⁸ We had heard of the city's glory,
   but now we have seen it ourselves—
   the city of the LORD of Heaven's Armies.
 It is the city of our God;
   he will make it safe forever.   *Interlude*

⁹ O God, we meditate on your unfailing love
   as we worship in your Temple.
¹⁰ As your name deserves, O God,
   you will be praised to the ends of the earth.
   Your strong right hand is filled with victory.
¹¹ Let the people on Mount Zion rejoice.
   Let all the towns of Judah be glad
   because of your justice.

¹² Go, inspect the city of Jerusalem.
    Walk around and count the many towers.
¹³ Take note of the fortified walls,
    and tour all the citadels,
that you may describe them
    to future generations.
¹⁴ For that is what God is like.
    He is our God forever and ever,
    and he will guide us until we die.

🔥 PSALM 49

For the choir director: A psalm of the descendants of Korah.

¹ Listen to this, all you people!
    Pay attention, everyone in the world!
² High and low,
    rich and poor—listen!
³ For my words are wise,
    and my thoughts are filled with insight.
⁴ I listen carefully to many proverbs
    and solve riddles with inspiration from a harp.

⁵ Why should I fear when trouble comes,
    when enemies surround me?
⁶ They trust in their wealth
    and boast of great riches.

⁷ Yet they cannot redeem themselves from death
     by paying a ransom to God.
⁸ Redemption does not come so easily,
     for no one can ever pay enough
⁹ to live forever
     and never see the grave.

¹⁰ Those who are wise must finally die,
     just like the foolish and senseless,
     leaving all their wealth behind.
¹¹ The grave is their eternal home,
     where they will stay forever.
  They may name their estates after
          themselves,
¹²   but their fame will not last.
     They will die, just like animals.
¹³ This is the fate of fools,
     though they are remembered as being wise.

Interlude

¹⁴ Like sheep, they are led to the grave,
     where death will be their shepherd.
  In the morning the godly will rule over them.
     Their bodies will rot in the grave,
     far from their grand estates.

¹⁵ But as for me, God will redeem my life.
    He will snatch me from the power of the grave.

Interlude

¹⁶ So don't be dismayed when the wicked grow rich
    and their homes become ever more splendid.
¹⁷ For when they die, they take nothing with them.
    Their wealth will not follow them into the grave.
¹⁸ In this life they consider themselves fortunate
    and are applauded for their success.
¹⁹ But they will die like all before them
    and never again see the light of day.
²⁰ People who boast of their wealth don't understand;
    they will die, just like animals.

❦ PSALM 50

A psalm of Asaph.

¹ The LORD, the Mighty One, is God,
    and he has spoken;
  he has summoned all humanity
    from where the sun rises to where it sets.
² From Mount Zion, the perfection of beauty,
    God shines in glorious radiance.
³ Our God approaches,
    and he is not silent.

Fire devours everything in his way,
  and a great storm rages around him.
⁴ He calls on the heavens above and earth below
  to witness the judgment of his people.
⁵ "Bring my faithful people to me—
  those who made a covenant with me by giving
    sacrifices."
⁶ Then let the heavens proclaim his justice,
  for God himself will be the judge.   *Interlude*

⁷ "O my people, listen as I speak.
  Here are my charges against you, O Israel:
  I am God, your God!
⁸ I have no complaint about your sacrifices
  or the burnt offerings you constantly offer.
⁹ But I do not need the bulls from your barns
  or the goats from your pens.
¹⁰ For all the animals of the forest are mine,
  and I own the cattle on a thousand hills.
¹¹ I know every bird on the mountains,
  and all the animals of the field are mine.
¹² If I were hungry, I would not tell you,
  for all the world is mine and everything in it.
¹³ Do I eat the meat of bulls?
  Do I drink the blood of goats?

¹⁴ Make thankfulness your sacrifice to God,
  and keep the vows you made to the
    Most High.
¹⁵ Then call on me when you are in trouble,
  and I will rescue you,
  and you will give me glory."

¹⁶ But God says to the wicked:
  "Why bother reciting my decrees
  and pretending to obey my covenant?
¹⁷ For you refuse my discipline
  and treat my words like trash.
¹⁸ When you see thieves, you approve of them,
  and you spend your time with adulterers.
¹⁹ Your mouth is filled with wickedness,
  and your tongue is full of lies.
²⁰ You sit around and slander your brother—
  your own mother's son.
²¹ While you did all this, I remained silent,
  and you thought I didn't care.
  But now I will rebuke you,
  listing all my charges against you.
²² Repent, all of you who forget me,
  or I will tear you apart,
  and no one will help you.

²³ But giving thanks is a sacrifice that truly honors me.
　　If you keep to my path,
　　I will reveal to you the salvation of God."

✳ PROVERBS 10

The proverbs of Solomon:

A wise child brings joy to a father;
　　a foolish child brings grief to a mother.

² Tainted wealth has no lasting value,
　　but right living can save your life.

³ The LORD will not let the godly go hungry,
　　but he refuses to satisfy the craving of the
　　　wicked.

⁴ Lazy people are soon poor;
　　hard workers get rich.

⁵ A wise youth harvests in the summer,
　　but one who sleeps during harvest is a disgrace.

⁶ The godly are showered with blessings;
　　the words of the wicked conceal violent
　　　intentions.

⁷ We have happy memories of the godly,
　　but the name of a wicked person rots away.

8 The wise are glad to be instructed,
   but babbling fools fall flat on their faces.

9 People with integrity walk safely,
   but those who follow crooked paths will
      be exposed.

10 People who wink at wrong cause trouble,
   but a bold reproof promotes peace.

11 The words of the godly are a life-giving fountain;
   the words of the wicked conceal violent
      intentions.

12 Hatred stirs up quarrels,
   but love makes up for all offenses.

13 Wise words come from the lips of people with
      understanding,
   but those lacking sense will be beaten with a rod.

14 Wise people treasure knowledge,
   but the babbling of a fool invites disaster.

15 The wealth of the rich is their fortress;
   the poverty of the poor is their destruction.

16 The earnings of the godly enhance their lives,
   but evil people squander their money on sin.

¹⁷ People who accept discipline are on the pathway
        to life,
    but those who ignore correction will go astray.

¹⁸ Hiding hatred makes you a liar;
    slandering others makes you a fool.

¹⁹ Too much talk leads to sin.
    Be sensible and keep your mouth shut.

²⁰ The words of the godly are like sterling silver;
    the heart of a fool is worthless.

²¹ The words of the godly encourage many,
    but fools are destroyed by their lack of
        common sense.

²² The blessing of the LORD makes a person rich,
    and he adds no sorrow with it.

²³ Doing wrong is fun for a fool,
    but living wisely brings pleasure to the sensible.

²⁴ The fears of the wicked will be fulfilled;
    the hopes of the godly will be granted.

²⁵ When the storms of life come, the wicked are
        whirled away,
    but the godly have a lasting foundation.

²⁶ Lazy people irritate their employers,
   like vinegar to the teeth or smoke in the eyes.

²⁷ Fear of the LORD lengthens one's life,
   but the years of the wicked are cut short.

²⁸ The hopes of the godly result in happiness,
   but the expectations of the wicked come to
      nothing.

²⁹ The way of the LORD is a stronghold to those
      with integrity,
   but it destroys the wicked.

³⁰ The godly will never be disturbed,
   but the wicked will be removed from the land.

³¹ The mouth of the godly person gives wise advice,
   but the tongue that deceives will be cut off.

³² The lips of the godly speak helpful words,
   but the mouth of the wicked speaks perverse
      words.

🔥 PSALM 51

For the choir director: A psalm of David, regarding the time Nathan the prophet came to him after David had committed adultery with Bathsheba.

1 Have mercy on me, O God,
    because of your unfailing love.
Because of your great compassion,
    blot out the stain of my sins.
2 Wash me clean from my guilt.
    Purify me from my sin.
3 For I recognize my rebellion;
    it haunts me day and night.
4 Against you, and you alone, have I sinned;
    I have done what is evil in your sight.
You will be proved right in what you say,
    and your judgment against me is just.
5 For I was born a sinner—
    yes, from the moment my mother conceived me.
6 But you desire honesty from the womb,
    teaching me wisdom even there.

7 Purify me from my sins, and I will be clean;
    wash me, and I will be whiter than snow.

⁸ Oh, give me back my joy again;
   you have broken me—
   now let me rejoice.
⁹ Don't keep looking at my sins.
   Remove the stain of my guilt.
¹⁰ Create in me a clean heart, O God.
   Renew a loyal spirit within me.
¹¹ Do not banish me from your presence,
   and don't take your Holy Spirit from me.

¹² Restore to me the joy of your salvation,
   and make me willing to obey you.
¹³ Then I will teach your ways to rebels,
   and they will return to you.
¹⁴ Forgive me for shedding blood, O God who saves;
   then I will joyfully sing of your forgiveness.
¹⁵ Unseal my lips, O Lord,
   that my mouth may praise you.

¹⁶ You do not desire a sacrifice, or I would offer one.
   You do not want a burnt offering.
¹⁷ The sacrifice you desire is a broken spirit.
   You will not reject a broken and repentant heart,
      O God.
¹⁸ Look with favor on Zion and help her;
   rebuild the walls of Jerusalem.

¹⁹ Then you will be pleased with sacrifices offered in
the right spirit—
with burnt offerings and whole burnt offerings.
Then bulls will again be sacrificed on
your altar.

❦ PSALM 52

*For the choir director: A psalm of David, regarding the time Doeg the
Edomite said to Saul, "David has gone to see Ahimelech."*

¹ Why do you boast about your crimes, great warrior?
Don't you realize God's justice continues forever?
² All day long you plot destruction.
Your tongue cuts like a sharp razor;
you're an expert at telling lies.
³ You love evil more than good
and lies more than truth. *Interlude*

⁴ You love to destroy others with your words,
you liar!
⁵ But God will strike you down once and for all.
He will pull you from your home
and uproot you from the land of the living. *Interlude*

⁶ The righteous will see it and be amazed.
They will laugh and say,

7 "Look what happens to mighty warriors
   who do not trust in God.
They trust their wealth instead
   and grow more and more bold in their
      wickedness."

8 But I am like an olive tree, thriving in the house
   of God.
   I will always trust in God's unfailing love.
9 I will praise you forever, O God,
   for what you have done.
   I will trust in your good name
   in the presence of your faithful people.

🔥 PSALM 53

For the choir director: A meditation; a psalm of David.

1 Only fools say in their hearts,
   "There is no God."
They are corrupt, and their actions are evil;
   not one of them does good!

2 God looks down from heaven
   on the entire human race;
he looks to see if anyone is truly wise,
   if anyone seeks God.

³ But no, all have turned away;
  all have become corrupt.
No one does good,
  not a single one!

⁴ Will those who do evil never learn?
  They eat up my people like bread
  and wouldn't think of praying to God.
⁵ Terror will grip them,
  terror like they have never known before.
God will scatter the bones of your enemies.
  You will put them to shame, for God has
  rejected them.

⁶ Who will come from Mount Zion to rescue
  Israel?
When God restores his people,
  Jacob will shout with joy, and Israel will
  rejoice.

❦ PSALM 54

For the choir director: A psalm of David, regarding the time the Ziphites came and said to Saul, "We know where David is hiding." To be accompanied by stringed instruments.

¹ Come with great power, O God, and rescue me!
  Defend me with your might.

² Listen to my prayer, O God.
  Pay attention to my plea.
³ For strangers are attacking me;
  violent people are trying to kill me.
  They care nothing for God.   *Interlude*

⁴ But God is my helper.
  The Lord keeps me alive!
⁵ May the evil plans of my enemies be turned
      against them.
  Do as you promised and put an end to them.

⁶ I will sacrifice a voluntary offering to you;
  I will praise your name, O LORD,
    for it is good.
⁷ For you have rescued me from my troubles
  and helped me to triumph over my enemies.

❦ PSALM 55

For the choir director: A psalm of David, to be accompanied by stringed
instruments.

¹ Listen to my prayer, O God.
  Do not ignore my cry for help!
² Please listen and answer me,
  for I am overwhelmed by my troubles.

³ My enemies shout at me,
    making loud and wicked threats.
  They bring trouble on me
    and angrily hunt me down.

⁴ My heart pounds in my chest.
    The terror of death assaults me.
⁵ Fear and trembling overwhelm me,
    and I can't stop shaking.
⁶ Oh, that I had wings like a dove;
    then I would fly away and rest!
⁷ I would fly far away
    to the quiet of the wilderness.   *Interlude*
⁸ How quickly I would escape—
    far from this wild storm of hatred.

⁹ Confuse them, Lord, and frustrate their plans,
    for I see violence and conflict in the city.
¹⁰ Its walls are patrolled day and night against
        invaders,
    but the real danger is wickedness within the city.
¹¹ Everything is falling apart;
    threats and cheating are rampant in the streets.

¹² It is not an enemy who taunts me—
    I could bear that.

It is not my foes who so arrogantly insult me—
    I could have hidden from them.
¹³ Instead, it is you—my equal,
    my companion and close friend.
¹⁴ What good fellowship we once enjoyed
    as we walked together to the house of God.

¹⁵ Let death stalk my enemies;
    let the grave swallow them alive,
    for evil makes its home within them.

¹⁶ But I will call on God,
    and the LORD will rescue me.
¹⁷ Morning, noon, and night
    I cry out in my distress,
    and the LORD hears my voice.
¹⁸ He ransoms me and keeps me safe
    from the battle waged against me,
    though many still oppose me.
¹⁹ God, who has ruled forever,
    will hear me and humble them.   *Interlude*
For my enemies refuse to change their ways;
    they do not fear God.

²⁰ As for my companion, he betrayed his friends;
    he broke his promises.

21 His words are as smooth as butter,
      but in his heart is war.
   His words are as soothing as lotion,
      but underneath are daggers!

22 Give your burdens to the LORD,
      and he will take care of you.
   He will not permit the godly to slip and fall.

23 But you, O God, will send the wicked
      down to the pit of destruction.
   Murderers and liars will die young,
      but I am trusting you to save me.

✳ PROVERBS 11

1 The LORD detests the use of dishonest scales,
      but he delights in accurate weights.

2 Pride leads to disgrace,
      but with humility comes wisdom.

3 Honesty guides good people;
      dishonesty destroys treacherous people.

4 Riches won't help on the day of judgment,
      but right living can save you from death.

⁵ The godly are directed by honesty;
   the wicked fall beneath their load of sin.

⁶ The godliness of good people rescues them;
   the ambition of treacherous people traps them.

⁷ When the wicked die, their hopes die with them,
   for they rely on their own feeble strength.

⁸ The godly are rescued from trouble,
   and it falls on the wicked instead.

⁹ With their words, the godless destroy
      their friends,
   but knowledge will rescue the righteous.

¹⁰ The whole city celebrates when the godly succeed;
   they shout for joy when the wicked die.

¹¹ Upright citizens are good for a city and make
      it prosper,
   but the talk of the wicked tears it apart.

¹² It is foolish to belittle one's neighbor;
   a sensible person keeps quiet.

¹³ A gossip goes around telling secrets,
   but those who are trustworthy can keep
      a confidence.

¹⁴ Without wise leadership, a nation falls;
    there is safety in having many advisers.

¹⁵ There's danger in putting up security for a
        stranger's debt;
    it's safer not to guarantee another person's debt.

¹⁶ A gracious woman gains respect,
    but ruthless men gain only wealth.

¹⁷ Your kindness will reward you,
    but your cruelty will destroy you.

¹⁸ Evil people get rich for the moment,
    but the reward of the godly will last.

¹⁹ Godly people find life;
    evil people find death.

²⁰ The LORD detests people with crooked hearts,
    but he delights in those with integrity.

²¹ Evil people will surely be punished,
    but the children of the godly will go free.

²² A beautiful woman who lacks discretion
    is like a gold ring in a pig's snout.

²³ The godly can look forward to a reward,
    while the wicked can expect only judgment.

²⁴ Give freely and become more wealthy;
    be stingy and lose everything.

²⁵ The generous will prosper;
    those who refresh others will themselves be
        refreshed.

²⁶ People curse those who hoard their grain,
    but they bless the one who sells in time
        of need.

²⁷ If you search for good, you will find favor;
    but if you search for evil, it will find you!

²⁸ Trust in your money and down you go!
    But the godly flourish like leaves in spring.

²⁹ Those who bring trouble on their families inherit
        the wind.
    The fool will be a servant to the wise.

³⁰ The seeds of good deeds become a tree of life;
    a wise person wins friends.

³¹ If the righteous are rewarded here on earth,
    what will happen to wicked sinners?

❧ PSALM 56

For the choir director: A psalm of David, regarding the time the Philistines seized him in Gath. To be sung to the tune "Dove on Distant Oaks."

1 O God, have mercy on me,
    for people are hounding me.
    My foes attack me all day long.
2 I am constantly hounded by those who
        slander me,
    and many are boldly attacking me.
3 But when I am afraid,
    I will put my trust in you.
4 I praise God for what he has promised.
    I trust in God, so why should I be afraid?
    What can mere mortals do to me?

5 They are always twisting what I say;
    they spend their days plotting to harm me.
6 They come together to spy on me—
    watching my every step, eager to kill me.
7 Don't let them get away with their
        wickedness;
    in your anger, O God, bring them down.

⁸ You keep track of all my sorrows.

> You have collected all my tears in your bottle.
> You have recorded each one in your book.

⁹ My enemies will retreat when I call to you for help.

> This I know: God is on my side!

¹⁰ I praise God for what he has promised;

> yes, I praise the Lord for what he has promised.

¹¹ I trust in God, so why should I be afraid?

> What can mere mortals do to me?

¹² I will fulfill my vows to you, O God,

> and will offer a sacrifice of thanks for your help.

¹³ For you have rescued me from death;

> you have kept my feet from slipping.

So now I can walk in your presence, O God,

> in your life-giving light.

❦ PSALM 57

For the choir director: A psalm of David, regarding the time he fled from Saul and went into the cave. To be sung to the tune "Do Not Destroy!"

¹ Have mercy on me, O God, have mercy!

> I look to you for protection.

I will hide beneath the shadow of your wings

> until the danger passes by.

² I cry out to God Most High,
    to God who will fulfill his purpose for me.
³ He will send help from heaven to
        rescue me,
    disgracing those who hound me.   *Interlude*
  My God will send forth his unfailing love and
        faithfulness.

⁴ I am surrounded by fierce lions
    who greedily devour human prey—
  whose teeth pierce like spears and arrows,
    and whose tongues cut like swords.

⁵ Be exalted, O God, above the highest heavens!
    May your glory shine over all the earth.

⁶ My enemies have set a trap for me.
    I am weary from distress.
  They have dug a deep pit in my path,
    but they themselves have fallen into it.   *Interlude*

⁷ My heart is confident in you, O God;
    my heart is confident.
    No wonder I can sing your praises!
⁸ Wake up, my heart!
    Wake up, O lyre and harp!
    I will wake the dawn with my song.

⁹ I will thank you, Lord, among all the people.
   I will sing your praises among the nations.
¹⁰ For your unfailing love is as high as the heavens.
   Your faithfulness reaches to the clouds.

¹¹ Be exalted, O God, above the highest heavens.
   May your glory shine over all the earth.

🔥 PSALM 58

For the choir director: A psalm of David, to be sung to the tune "Do Not Destroy!"

¹ Justice—do you rulers know the meaning of the
      word?
   Do you judge the people fairly?
² No! You plot injustice in your hearts.
   You spread violence throughout the land.
³ These wicked people are born sinners;
   even from birth they have lied and gone their
      own way.
⁴ They spit venom like deadly snakes;
   they are like cobras that refuse to listen,
⁵ ignoring the tunes of the snake charmers,
   no matter how skillfully they play.

⁶ Break off their fangs, O God!
   Smash the jaws of these lions, O LORD!

7 May they disappear like water into thirsty ground.
  Make their weapons useless in their hands.
8 May they be like snails that dissolve into slime,
  like a stillborn child who will never see the sun.
9 God will sweep them away, both young and old,
  faster than a pot heats over burning thorns.

10 The godly will rejoice when they see injustice
   avenged.
   They will wash their feet in the blood of the
   wicked.
11 Then at last everyone will say,
   "There truly is a reward for those who live for God;
   surely there is a God who judges justly here on
   earth."

🌱 PSALM 59

For the choir director: A psalm of David, regarding the time Saul sent
soldiers to watch David's house in order to kill him. To be sung to the
tune "Do Not Destroy!"

1 Rescue me from my enemies, O God.
  Protect me from those who have come to
     destroy me.
2 Rescue me from these criminals;
  save me from these murderers.

³ They have set an ambush for me.
  Fierce enemies are out there waiting, LORD,
  though I have not sinned or offended them.
⁴ I have done nothing wrong,
  yet they prepare to attack me.
  Wake up! See what is happening and
    help me!
⁵ O LORD God of Heaven's Armies, the
    God of Israel,
  wake up and punish those hostile nations.
  Show no mercy to wicked traitors.   *Interlude*

⁶ They come out at night,
  snarling like vicious dogs
  as they prowl the streets.
⁷ Listen to the filth that comes from their mouths;
  their words cut like swords.
  "After all, who can hear us?" they sneer.
⁸ But LORD, you laugh at them.
  You scoff at all the hostile nations.
⁹ You are my strength; I wait for you to rescue me,
  for you, O God, are my fortress.
¹⁰ In his unfailing love, my God will stand with me.
  He will let me look down in triumph on all my
    enemies.

¹¹ Don't kill them, for my people soon forget
        such lessons;
    stagger them with your power, and bring
        them to their knees,
    O Lord our shield.
¹² Because of the sinful things they say,
        because of the evil that is on their lips,
    let them be captured by their pride,
        their curses, and their lies.
¹³ Destroy them in your anger!
        Wipe them out completely!
    Then the whole world will know
        that God reigns in Israel.   *Interlude*

¹⁴ My enemies come out at night,
        snarling like vicious dogs
        as they prowl the streets.
¹⁵ They scavenge for food
        but go to sleep unsatisfied.

¹⁶ But as for me, I will sing about your power.
        Each morning I will sing with joy about your
        unfailing love.
    For you have been my refuge,
        a place of safety when I am in distress.

DAY 12   PSALM 59

¹⁷ O my Strength, to you I sing praises,
    for you, O God, are my refuge,
        the God who shows me unfailing love.

❦ PSALM 60

*For the choir director: A psalm of David useful for teaching, regarding
the time David fought Aram-naharaim and Aram-zobah, and Joab
returned and killed 12,000 Edomites in the Valley of Salt. To be sung
to the tune "Lily of the Testimony."*

¹ You have rejected us, O God, and broken our
        defenses.
    You have been angry with us; now restore us
        to your favor.
² You have shaken our land and split it open.
    Seal the cracks, for the land trembles.
³ You have been very hard on us,
    making us drink wine that sent us reeling.
⁴ But you have raised a banner for those who
        fear you—
    a rallying point in the face of attack.   *Interlude*

⁵ Now rescue your beloved people.
    Answer and save us by your power.
⁶ God has promised this by his holiness:
    "I will divide up Shechem with joy.
        I will measure out the valley of Succoth.

⁷ Gilead is mine,
    and Manasseh, too.
  Ephraim, my helmet, will produce my warriors,
    and Judah, my scepter, will produce my kings.
⁸ But Moab, my washbasin, will become my servant,
    and I will wipe my feet on Edom
    and shout in triumph over Philistia."

⁹ Who will bring me into the fortified city?
    Who will bring me victory over Edom?
¹⁰ Have you rejected us, O God?
    Will you no longer march with our armies?
¹¹ Oh, please help us against our enemies,
    for all human help is useless.
¹² With God's help we will do mighty things,
    for he will trample down our foes.

✳ PROVERBS 12

¹ To learn, you must love discipline;
    it is stupid to hate correction.

² The LORD approves of those who are good,
    but he condemns those who plan wickedness.

³ Wickedness never brings stability,
    but the godly have deep roots.

⁴ A worthy wife is a crown for her husband,
   but a disgraceful woman is like cancer in
      his bones.

⁵ The plans of the godly are just;
   the advice of the wicked is treacherous.

⁶ The words of the wicked are like a murderous
      ambush,
   but the words of the godly save lives.

⁷ The wicked die and disappear,
   but the family of the godly stands firm.

⁸ A sensible person wins admiration,
   but a warped mind is despised.

⁹ Better to be an ordinary person with a servant
   than to be self-important but have no food.

¹⁰ The godly care for their animals,
   but the wicked are always cruel.

¹¹ A hard worker has plenty of food,
   but a person who chases fantasies has
      no sense.

¹² Thieves are jealous of each other's loot,
   but the godly are well rooted and bear their
      own fruit.

¹³ The wicked are trapped by their own words,
   but the godly escape such trouble.

¹⁴ Wise words bring many benefits,
   and hard work brings rewards.

¹⁵ Fools think their own way is right,
   but the wise listen to others.

¹⁶ A fool is quick-tempered,
   but a wise person stays calm when insulted.

¹⁷ An honest witness tells the truth;
   a false witness tells lies.

¹⁸ Some people make cutting remarks,
   but the words of the wise bring healing.

¹⁹ Truthful words stand the test of time,
   but lies are soon exposed.

²⁰ Deceit fills hearts that are plotting evil;
   joy fills hearts that are planning peace!

²¹ No harm comes to the godly,
   but the wicked have their fill of trouble.

²² The LORD detests lying lips,
   but he delights in those who tell the truth.

²³ The wise don't make a show of their knowledge,
   but fools broadcast their foolishness.

²⁴ Work hard and become a leader;
   be lazy and become a slave.

²⁵ Worry weighs a person down;
   an encouraging word cheers a person up.

²⁶ The godly give good advice to their friends;
   the wicked lead them astray.

²⁷ Lazy people don't even cook the game they catch,
   but the diligent make use of everything they
      find.

²⁸ The way of the godly leads to life;
   that path does not lead to death.

DAY THIRTEEN

🕯 PSALM 61

For the choir director: A psalm of David, to be accompanied by stringed instruments.

¹ O God, listen to my cry!
　　Hear my prayer!
² From the ends of the earth,
　　I cry to you for help
　　when my heart is overwhelmed.
　Lead me to the towering rock of safety,
³ 　for you are my safe refuge,
　　a fortress where my enemies cannot reach me.
⁴ Let me live forever in your sanctuary,
　　safe beneath the shelter of your wings!　　*Interlude*

⁵ For you have heard my vows, O God.
　　You have given me an inheritance reserved for
　　　　those who fear your name.
⁶ Add many years to the life of the king!
　　May his years span the generations!
⁷ May he reign under God's protection forever.
　　May your unfailing love and faithfulness watch
　　　　over him.

⁸ Then I will sing praises to your name forever
as I fulfill my vows each day.

🕯 PSALM 62

For Jeduthun, the choir director: A psalm of David.

¹ I wait quietly before God,
for my victory comes from him.
² He alone is my rock and my salvation,
my fortress where I will never be shaken.

³ So many enemies against one man—
all of them trying to kill me.
To them I'm just a broken-down wall
or a tottering fence.
⁴ They plan to topple me from my high position.
They delight in telling lies about me.
They praise me to my face
but curse me in their hearts. *Interlude*

⁵ Let all that I am wait quietly before God,
for my hope is in him.
⁶ He alone is my rock and my salvation,
my fortress where I will not be shaken.
⁷ My victory and honor come from God alone.
He is my refuge, a rock where no enemy can
reach me.

⁸ O my people, trust in him at all times.
  Pour out your heart to him,
  for God is our refuge.   *Interlude*

⁹ Common people are as worthless as a puff of wind,
  and the powerful are not what they appear to be.
 If you weigh them on the scales,
  together they are lighter than a breath of air.

¹⁰ Don't make your living by extortion
  or put your hope in stealing.
 And if your wealth increases,
  don't make it the center of your life.

¹¹ God has spoken plainly,
  and I have heard it many times:
 Power, O God, belongs to you;
¹²   unfailing love, O Lord, is yours.
 Surely you repay all people
  according to what they have done.

🕯 PSALM 63

A psalm of David, regarding a time when David was in the wilderness of Judah.

¹ O God, you are my God;
  I earnestly search for you.

My soul thirsts for you;
    my whole body longs for you
in this parched and weary land
    where there is no water.
2 I have seen you in your sanctuary
    and gazed upon your power and glory.
3 Your unfailing love is better than life itself;
    how I praise you!
4 I will praise you as long as I live,
    lifting up my hands to you in prayer.
5 You satisfy me more than the richest feast.
    I will praise you with songs of joy.

6 I lie awake thinking of you,
    meditating on you through the night.
7 Because you are my helper,
    I sing for joy in the shadow of your wings.
8 I cling to you;
    your strong right hand holds me securely.

9 But those plotting to destroy me will come
        to ruin.
    They will go down into the depths of the earth.
10 They will die by the sword
    and become the food of jackals.

11 But the king will rejoice in God.
  All who swear to tell the truth will praise him,
  while liars will be silenced.

🔥 PSALM 64

For the choir director: A psalm of David.

1 O God, listen to my complaint.
  Protect my life from my enemies' threats.
2 Hide me from the plots of this evil mob,
  from this gang of wrongdoers.
3 They sharpen their tongues like swords
  and aim their bitter words like arrows.
4 They shoot from ambush at the innocent,
  attacking suddenly and fearlessly.
5 They encourage each other to do evil
  and plan how to set their traps in secret.
  "Who will ever notice?" they ask.
6 As they plot their crimes, they say,
  "We have devised the perfect plan!"
  Yes, the human heart and mind are cunning.

7 But God himself will shoot them with
    his arrows,
  suddenly striking them down.

⁸ Their own tongues will ruin them,
    and all who see them will shake their heads
        in scorn.
⁹ Then everyone will be afraid;
    they will proclaim the mighty acts of God
    and realize all the amazing things he does.
¹⁰ The godly will rejoice in the LORD
    and find shelter in him.
  And those who do what is right
    will praise him.

🔥 PSALM 65

For the choir director: A song. A psalm of David.

¹ What mighty praise, O God,
    belongs to you in Zion.
  We will fulfill our vows to you,
²   for you answer our prayers.
    All of us must come to you.
³ Though we are overwhelmed by our sins,
    you forgive them all.
⁴ What joy for those you choose to bring near,
    those who live in your holy courts.
  What festivities await us
    inside your holy Temple.

⁵ You faithfully answer our prayers with
      awesome deeds,
    O God our savior.
  You are the hope of everyone on earth,
      even those who sail on distant seas.
⁶ You formed the mountains by your power
    and armed yourself with mighty
        strength.
⁷ You quieted the raging oceans
    with their pounding waves
    and silenced the shouting of the nations.
⁸ Those who live at the ends of the earth
    stand in awe of your wonders.
  From where the sun rises to where it sets,
      you inspire shouts of joy.

⁹ You take care of the earth and water it,
      making it rich and fertile.
  The river of God has plenty of water;
      it provides a bountiful harvest of grain,
      for you have ordered it so.
¹⁰ You drench the plowed ground with rain,
      melting the clods and leveling the ridges.
  You soften the earth with showers
      and bless its abundant crops.

¹¹ You crown the year with a bountiful harvest;
    even the hard pathways overflow with abundance.
¹² The grasslands of the wilderness become a lush
      pasture,
    and the hillsides blossom with joy.
¹³ The meadows are clothed with flocks of sheep,
    and the valleys are carpeted with grain.
    They all shout and sing for joy!

✳ PROVERBS 13

¹ A wise child accepts a parent's discipline;
    a mocker refuses to listen to correction.

² Wise words will win you a good meal,
    but treacherous people have an appetite for
      violence.

³ Those who control their tongue will have a long life;
    opening your mouth can ruin everything.

⁴ Lazy people want much but get little,
    but those who work hard will prosper.

⁵ The godly hate lies;
    the wicked cause shame and disgrace.

⁶ Godliness guards the path of the blameless,
    but the evil are misled by sin.

7 Some who are poor pretend to be rich;
    others who are rich pretend to be poor.

8 The rich can pay a ransom for their lives,
    but the poor won't even get threatened.

9 The life of the godly is full of light and joy,
    but the light of the wicked will be snuffed out.

10 Pride leads to conflict;
    those who take advice are wise.

11 Wealth from get-rich-quick schemes quickly
        disappears;
    wealth from hard work grows over time.

12 Hope deferred makes the heart sick,
    but a dream fulfilled is a tree of life.

13 People who despise advice are asking for trouble;
    those who respect a command will succeed.

14 The instruction of the wise is like a life-giving
        fountain;
    those who accept it avoid the snares of death.

15 A person with good sense is respected;
    a treacherous person is headed for destruction.

16 Wise people think before they act;
    fools don't—and even brag about their foolishness.

¹⁷ An unreliable messenger stumbles into trouble,
    but a reliable messenger brings healing.

¹⁸ If you ignore criticism, you will end in poverty
        and disgrace;
    if you accept correction, you will be honored.

¹⁹ It is pleasant to see dreams come true,
    but fools refuse to turn from evil to attain them.

²⁰ Walk with the wise and become wise;
    associate with fools and get in trouble.

²¹ Trouble chases sinners,
    while blessings reward the righteous.

²² Good people leave an inheritance to their
        grandchildren,
    but the sinner's wealth passes to the godly.

²³ A poor person's farm may produce much food,
    but injustice sweeps it all away.

²⁴ Those who spare the rod of discipline hate their
        children.
    Those who love their children care enough
        to discipline them.

²⁵ The godly eat to their hearts' content,
    but the belly of the wicked goes hungry.

🪶 PSALM 66

For the choir director: A song. A psalm.

¹ Shout joyful praises to God, all the earth!
²   Sing about the glory of his name!
    Tell the world how glorious he is.
³ Say to God, "How awesome are your deeds!
    Your enemies cringe before your mighty power.
⁴ Everything on earth will worship you;
    they will sing your praises,
    shouting your name in glorious songs." *Interlude*

⁵ Come and see what our God has done,
    what awesome miracles he performs
      for people!
⁶ He made a dry path through the Red Sea,
    and his people went across on foot.
    There we rejoiced in him.
⁷ For by his great power he rules forever.
    He watches every movement of the nations;
    let no rebel rise in defiance. *Interlude*

⁸ Let the whole world bless our God
    and loudly sing his praises.

⁹ Our lives are in his hands,
   and he keeps our feet from stumbling.
¹⁰ You have tested us, O God;
   you have purified us like silver.
¹¹ You captured us in your net
   and laid the burden of slavery on our backs.
¹² Then you put a leader over us.
   We went through fire and flood,
   but you brought us to a place of great
      abundance.

¹³ Now I come to your Temple with burnt offerings
   to fulfill the vows I made to you—
¹⁴ yes, the sacred vows that I made
   when I was in deep trouble.
¹⁵ That is why I am sacrificing burnt offerings to
      you—
   the best of my rams as a pleasing aroma,
   and a sacrifice of bulls and male goats.   *Interlude*

¹⁶ Come and listen, all you who fear God,
   and I will tell you what he did for me.
¹⁷ For I cried out to him for help,
   praising him as I spoke.
¹⁸ If I had not confessed the sin in my heart,
   the Lord would not have listened.

¹⁹ But God did listen!
    He paid attention to my prayer.
²⁰ Praise God, who did not ignore my prayer
    or withdraw his unfailing love from me.

🔥 PSALM 67

For the choir director: A song. A psalm, to be accompanied by stringed instruments.

¹ May God be merciful and bless us.
    May his face smile with favor on us.   *Interlude*

² May your ways be known throughout the earth,
    your saving power among people everywhere.
³ May the nations praise you, O God.
    Yes, may all the nations praise you.
⁴ Let the whole world sing for joy,
    because you govern the nations with justice
    and guide the people of the whole world.

                                          Interlude

⁵ May the nations praise you, O God.
    Yes, may all the nations praise you.
⁶ Then the earth will yield its harvests,
    and God, our God, will richly bless us.
⁷ Yes, God will bless us,
    and people all over the world will fear him.

🔥 PSALM 68

For the choir director: A song. A psalm of David.

¹ Rise up, O God, and scatter your enemies.
  Let those who hate God run for their lives.
² Blow them away like smoke.
  Melt them like wax in a fire.
  Let the wicked perish in the presence of God.
³ But let the godly rejoice.
  Let them be glad in God's presence.
  Let them be filled with joy.
⁴ Sing praises to God and to his name!
  Sing loud praises to him who rides the clouds.
 His name is the LORD—
  rejoice in his presence!

⁵ Father to the fatherless, defender of widows—
  this is God, whose dwelling is holy.
⁶ God places the lonely in families;
  he sets the prisoners free and gives them joy.
 But he makes the rebellious live in a sun-scorched
      land.

⁷ O God, when you led your people out from Egypt,
  when you marched through the dry wasteland,
                                      Interlude

⁸ the earth trembled, and the heavens poured
down rain
before you, the God of Sinai,
before God, the God of Israel.
⁹ You sent abundant rain, O God,
to refresh the weary land.
¹⁰ There your people finally settled,
and with a bountiful harvest, O God,
you provided for your needy people.

¹¹ The Lord gives the word,
and a great army brings the good news.
¹² Enemy kings and their armies flee,
while the women of Israel divide the plunder.
¹³ Even those who lived among the sheepfolds found
treasures—
doves with wings of silver
and feathers of gold.
¹⁴ The Almighty scattered the enemy kings
like a blowing snowstorm on Mount Zalmon.

¹⁵ The mountains of Bashan are majestic,
with many peaks stretching high into the sky.
¹⁶ Why do you look with envy, O rugged mountains,
at Mount Zion, where God has chosen to live,
where the LORD himself will live forever?

¹⁷ Surrounded by unnumbered thousands of chariots,
    the Lord came from Mount Sinai into his
        sanctuary.
¹⁸ When you ascended to the heights,
    you led a crowd of captives.
  You received gifts from the people,
    even from those who rebelled against you.
    Now the LORD God will live among us there.

¹⁹ Praise the Lord; praise God our savior!
    For each day he carries us in his arms.   *Interlude*
²⁰ Our God is a God who saves!
    The Sovereign LORD rescues us from death.

²¹ But God will smash the heads of his enemies,
    crushing the skulls of those who love their
        guilty ways.
²² The Lord says, "I will bring my enemies down
        from Bashan;
    I will bring them up from the depths of the sea.
²³ You, my people, will wash your feet in their blood,
    and even your dogs will get their share!"

²⁴ Your procession has come into view, O God—
    the procession of my God and King as he goes
        into the sanctuary.

²⁵ Singers are in front, musicians behind;
     between them are young women playing
       tambourines.
²⁶ Praise God, all you people of Israel;
     praise the LORD, the source of Israel's life.
²⁷ Look, the little tribe of Benjamin leads the way.
     Then comes a great throng of rulers from Judah
     and all the rulers of Zebulun and Naphtali.

²⁸ Summon your might, O God.
     Display your power, O God, as you have in
       the past.
²⁹ The kings of the earth are bringing tribute
     to your Temple in Jerusalem.
³⁰ Rebuke these enemy nations—
     these wild animals lurking in the reeds,
     this herd of bulls among the weaker calves.
   Make them bring bars of silver in humble tribute.
     Scatter the nations that delight in war.
³¹ Let Egypt come with gifts of precious metals;
     let Ethiopia bring tribute to God.
³² Sing to God, you kingdoms of the earth.
     Sing praises to the Lord.   *Interlude*
³³ Sing to the one who rides across the ancient heavens,
     his mighty voice thundering from the sky.

[34] Tell everyone about God's power.
   His majesty shines down on Israel;
      his strength is mighty in the heavens.
[35] God is awesome in his sanctuary.
   The God of Israel gives power and strength
      to his people.

Praise be to God!

🌿 PSALM 69

For the choir director: A psalm of David, to be sung to the tune "Lilies."

[1] Save me, O God,
   for the floodwaters are up to my neck.
[2] Deeper and deeper I sink into the mire;
   I can't find a foothold.
I am in deep water,
   and the floods overwhelm me.
[3] I am exhausted from crying for help;
   my throat is parched.
My eyes are swollen with weeping,
   waiting for my God to help me.
[4] Those who hate me without cause
   outnumber the hairs on my head.
Many enemies try to destroy me with lies,
   demanding that I give back what I didn't steal.

⁵ O God, you know how foolish I am;
   my sins cannot be hidden from you.
⁶ Don't let those who trust in you be ashamed
      because of me,
   O Sovereign LORD of Heaven's Armies.
 Don't let me cause them to be humiliated,
   O God of Israel.
⁷ For I endure insults for your sake;
   humiliation is written all over my face.
⁸ Even my own brothers pretend they don't know me;
   they treat me like a stranger.

⁹ Passion for your house has consumed me,
   and the insults of those who insult you have
      fallen on me.
¹⁰ When I weep and fast,
   they scoff at me.
¹¹ When I dress in burlap to show sorrow,
   they make fun of me.
¹² I am the favorite topic of town gossip,
   and all the drunks sing about me.

¹³ But I keep praying to you, LORD,
   hoping this time you will show me favor.
 In your unfailing love, O God,
   answer my prayer with your sure salvation.

¹⁴ Rescue me from the mud;
     don't let me sink any deeper!
  Save me from those who hate me,
     and pull me from these deep waters.
¹⁵ Don't let the floods overwhelm me,
     or the deep waters swallow me,
     or the pit of death devour me.

¹⁶ Answer my prayers, O LORD,
     for your unfailing love is wonderful.
  Take care of me,
     for your mercy is so plentiful.
¹⁷ Don't hide from your servant;
     answer me quickly, for I am in deep trouble!
¹⁸ Come and redeem me;
     free me from my enemies.

¹⁹ You know of my shame, scorn, and disgrace.
     You see all that my enemies are doing.
²⁰ Their insults have broken my heart,
     and I am in despair.
  If only one person would show some pity;
     if only one would turn and comfort me.
²¹ But instead, they give me poison for food;
     they offer me sour wine for my thirst.

²² Let the bountiful table set before them become
　　　a snare
　　and their prosperity become a trap.
²³ Let their eyes go blind so they cannot see,
　　and make their bodies shake continually.
²⁴ Pour out your fury on them;
　　consume them with your burning anger.
²⁵ Let their homes become desolate
　　and their tents be deserted.
²⁶ To the one you have punished, they add insult
　　　to injury;
　　they add to the pain of those you have hurt.
²⁷ Pile their sins up high,
　　and don't let them go free.
²⁸ Erase their names from the Book of Life;
　　don't let them be counted among the righteous.

²⁹ I am suffering and in pain.
　　Rescue me, O God, by your saving power.

³⁰ Then I will praise God's name with singing,
　　and I will honor him with thanksgiving.
³¹ For this will please the LORD more than sacrificing
　　　cattle,
　　more than presenting a bull with its horns and
　　　hooves.

³² The humble will see their God at work and
     be glad.
   Let all who seek God's help be encouraged.
³³ For the LORD hears the cries of the needy;
     he does not despise his imprisoned people.

³⁴ Praise him, O heaven and earth,
     the seas and all that move in them.
³⁵ For God will save Jerusalem
     and rebuild the towns of Judah.
   His people will live there
     and settle in their own land.
³⁶ The descendants of those who obey him will
     inherit the land,
     and those who love him will live there in safety.

PSALM 70

For the choir director: A psalm of David, asking God to remember him.

¹ Please, God, rescue me!
   Come quickly, LORD, and help me.
² May those who try to kill me
   be humiliated and put to shame.
   May those who take delight in my trouble
   be turned back in disgrace.

³ Let them be horrified by their shame,
    for they said, "Aha! We've got him now!"
⁴ But may all who search for you
    be filled with joy and gladness in you.
May those who love your salvation
    repeatedly shout, "God is great!"
⁵ But as for me, I am poor and needy;
    please hurry to my aid, O God.
You are my helper and my savior;
    O LORD, do not delay.

✳ PROVERBS 14

¹ A wise woman builds her home,
    but a foolish woman tears it down with her
        own hands.

² Those who follow the right path fear the LORD;
    those who take the wrong path despise him.

³ A fool's proud talk becomes a rod that beats him,
    but the words of the wise keep them safe.

⁴ Without oxen a stable stays clean,
    but you need a strong ox for a large harvest.

⁵ An honest witness does not lie;
    a false witness breathes lies.

⁶ A mocker seeks wisdom and never finds it,
    but knowledge comes easily to those with
        understanding.

⁷ Stay away from fools,
    for you won't find knowledge on their lips.

⁸ The prudent understand where they are going,
    but fools deceive themselves.

⁹ Fools make fun of guilt,
    but the godly acknowledge it and seek
        reconciliation.

¹⁰ Each heart knows its own bitterness,
    and no one else can fully share its joy.

¹¹ The house of the wicked will be destroyed,
    but the tent of the godly will flourish.

¹² There is a path before each person that
        seems right,
    but it ends in death.

¹³ Laughter can conceal a heavy heart,
    but when the laughter ends, the grief remains.

¹⁴ Backsliders get what they deserve;
    good people receive their reward.

¹⁵ Only simpletons believe everything they're told!
    The prudent carefully consider their steps.

¹⁶ The wise are cautious and avoid danger;
    fools plunge ahead with reckless confidence.

¹⁷ Short-tempered people do foolish things,
    and schemers are hated.

¹⁸ Simpletons are clothed with foolishness,
    but the prudent are crowned with knowledge.

¹⁹ Evil people will bow before good people;
    the wicked will bow at the gates of the godly.

²⁰ The poor are despised even by their neighbors,
    while the rich have many "friends."

²¹ It is a sin to belittle one's neighbor;
    blessed are those who help the poor.

²² If you plan to do evil, you will be lost;
    if you plan to do good, you will receive unfailing
      love and faithfulness.

²³ Work brings profit,
    but mere talk leads to poverty!

²⁴ Wealth is a crown for the wise;
    the effort of fools yields only foolishness.

²⁵ A truthful witness saves lives,
    but a false witness is a traitor.

²⁶ Those who fear the LORD are secure;
    he will be a refuge for their children.

²⁷ Fear of the LORD is a life-giving fountain;
    it offers escape from the snares of death.

²⁸ A growing population is a king's glory;
    a prince without subjects has nothing.

²⁹ People with understanding control their anger;
    a hot temper shows great foolishness.

³⁰ A peaceful heart leads to a healthy body;
    jealousy is like cancer in the bones.

³¹ Those who oppress the poor insult their Maker,
    but helping the poor honors him.

³² The wicked are crushed by disaster,
    but the godly have a refuge when they die.

³³ Wisdom is enshrined in an understanding heart;
    wisdom is not found among fools.

³⁴ Godliness makes a nation great,
    but sin is a disgrace to any people.

³⁵ A king rejoices in wise servants
    but is angry with those who disgrace him.

❦ PSALM 71

¹ O LORD, I have come to you for protection;
    don't let me be disgraced.
² Save me and rescue me,
    for you do what is right.
  Turn your ear to listen to me,
    and set me free.
³ Be my rock of safety
    where I can always hide.
  Give the order to save me,
    for you are my rock and my fortress.
⁴ My God, rescue me from the power of the wicked,
    from the clutches of cruel oppressors.
⁵ O Lord, you alone are my hope.
    I've trusted you, O LORD, from childhood.
⁶ Yes, you have been with me from birth;
    from my mother's womb you have cared for me.
    No wonder I am always praising you!

⁷ My life is an example to many,
    because you have been my strength and
      protection.

⁸ That is why I can never stop praising you;
   I declare your glory all day long.
⁹ And now, in my old age, don't set me aside.
   Don't abandon me when my strength is failing.
¹⁰ For my enemies are whispering against me.
   They are plotting together to kill me.
¹¹ They say, "God has abandoned him.
   Let's go and get him,
   for no one will help him now."

¹² O God, don't stay away.
   My God, please hurry to help me.
¹³ Bring disgrace and destruction on my accusers.
   Humiliate and shame those who want to
      harm me.
¹⁴ But I will keep on hoping for your help;
   I will praise you more and more.
¹⁵ I will tell everyone about your righteousness.
   All day long I will proclaim your saving power,
   though I am not skilled with words.
¹⁶ I will praise your mighty deeds, O Sovereign LORD.
   I will tell everyone that you alone are just.

¹⁷ O God, you have taught me from my earliest
      childhood,

and I constantly tell others about the wonderful
    things you do.
¹⁸ Now that I am old and gray,
    do not abandon me, O God.
  Let me proclaim your power to this new generation,
    your mighty miracles to all who come after me.

¹⁹ Your righteousness, O God, reaches to the highest
    heavens.
    You have done such wonderful things.
    Who can compare with you, O God?
²⁰ You have allowed me to suffer much hardship,
    but you will restore me to life again
    and lift me up from the depths of the earth.
²¹ You will restore me to even greater honor
    and comfort me once again.

²² Then I will praise you with music on the harp,
    because you are faithful to your promises,
        O my God.
  I will sing praises to you with a lyre,
    O Holy One of Israel.
²³ I will shout for joy and sing your praises,
    for you have ransomed me.
²⁴ I will tell about your righteous deeds
    all day long,

for everyone who tried to hurt me
  has been shamed and humiliated.

❦ PSALM 72

A psalm of Solomon.

¹ Give your love of justice to the king, O God,
  and righteousness to the king's son.
² Help him judge your people in the right way;
  let the poor always be treated fairly.
³ May the mountains yield prosperity for all,
  and may the hills be fruitful.
⁴ Help him to defend the poor,
  to rescue the children of the needy,
  and to crush their oppressors.
⁵ May they fear you as long as the sun shines,
  as long as the moon remains in the sky.
  Yes, forever!

⁶ May the king's rule be refreshing like spring rain
    on freshly cut grass,
  like the showers that water the earth.
⁷ May all the godly flourish during his reign.
  May there be abundant prosperity until the
    moon is no more.

⁸ May he reign from sea to sea,
  and from the Euphrates River to the ends
    of the earth.
⁹ Desert nomads will bow before him;
  his enemies will fall before him in the dust.
¹⁰ The western kings of Tarshish and other distant
      lands
  will bring him tribute.
The eastern kings of Sheba and Seba
  will bring him gifts.
¹¹ All kings will bow before him,
  and all nations will serve him.

¹² He will rescue the poor when they cry to him;
  he will help the oppressed, who have no one to
    defend them.
¹³ He feels pity for the weak and the needy,
  and he will rescue them.
¹⁴ He will redeem them from oppression and violence,
  for their lives are precious to him.

¹⁵ Long live the king!
  May the gold of Sheba be given to him.
May the people always pray for him
  and bless him all day long.

¹⁶ May there be abundant grain throughout the land,
    flourishing even on the hilltops.
  May the fruit trees flourish like the trees of Lebanon,
    and may the people thrive like grass in a field.
¹⁷ May the king's name endure forever;
    may it continue as long as the sun shines.
  May all nations be blessed through him
    and bring him praise.

¹⁸ Praise the LORD God, the God of Israel,
    who alone does such wonderful things.
¹⁹ Praise his glorious name forever!
    Let the whole earth be filled with his glory.
  Amen and amen!

²⁰ (This ends the prayers of David son of Jesse.)

BOOK THREE (PSALMS 73–89)

 **PSALM 73**
A psalm of Asaph.

¹ Truly God is good to Israel,
    to those whose hearts are pure.
² But as for me, I almost lost my footing.
    My feet were slipping, and I was almost gone.

³ For I envied the proud
    when I saw them prosper despite their wickedness.
⁴ They seem to live such painless lives;
    their bodies are so healthy and strong.
⁵ They don't have troubles like other people;
    they're not plagued with problems like
        everyone else.
⁶ They wear pride like a jeweled necklace
    and clothe themselves with cruelty.
⁷ These fat cats have everything
    their hearts could ever wish for!
⁸ They scoff and speak only evil;
    in their pride they seek to crush others.
⁹ They boast against the very heavens,
    and their words strut throughout the earth.
¹⁰ And so the people are dismayed and confused,
    drinking in all their words.
¹¹ "What does God know?" they ask.
    "Does the Most High even know what's
        happening?"
¹² Look at these wicked people—
    enjoying a life of ease while their riches multiply.

¹³ Did I keep my heart pure for nothing?
    Did I keep myself innocent for no reason?

¹⁴ I get nothing but trouble all day long;
   every morning brings me pain.

¹⁵ If I had really spoken this way to others,
   I would have been a traitor to your people.

¹⁶ So I tried to understand why the wicked prosper.
   But what a difficult task it is!

¹⁷ Then I went into your sanctuary, O God,
   and I finally understood the destiny of the
      wicked.

¹⁸ Truly, you put them on a slippery path
   and send them sliding over the cliff to
      destruction.

¹⁹ In an instant they are destroyed,
   completely swept away by terrors.

²⁰ When you arise, O Lord,
   you will laugh at their silly ideas
   as a person laughs at dreams in the morning.

²¹ Then I realized that my heart was bitter,
   and I was all torn up inside.

²² I was so foolish and ignorant—
   I must have seemed like a senseless animal to you.

²³ Yet I still belong to you;
   you hold my right hand.

²⁴ You guide me with your counsel,
   leading me to a glorious destiny.
²⁵ Whom have I in heaven but you?
   I desire you more than anything on earth.
²⁶ My health may fail, and my spirit may grow weak,
   but God remains the strength of my heart;
   he is mine forever.

²⁷ Those who desert him will perish,
   for you destroy those who abandon you.
²⁸ But as for me, how good it is to be near God!
   I have made the Sovereign LORD my shelter,
   and I will tell everyone about the wonderful
      things you do.

🕯 PSALM 74

A psalm of Asaph.

¹ O God, why have you rejected us so long?
   Why is your anger so intense against the sheep
      of your own pasture?
² Remember that we are the people you chose
      long ago,
   the tribe you redeemed as your own special
      possession!

And remember Jerusalem, your home here
    on earth.
³ Walk through the awful ruins of the city;
    see how the enemy has destroyed your
        sanctuary.

⁴ There your enemies shouted their victorious
        battle cries;
    there they set up their battle standards.
⁵ They swung their axes
    like woodcutters in a forest.
⁶ With axes and picks,
    they smashed the carved paneling.
⁷ They burned your sanctuary to the ground.
    They defiled the place that bears your name.
⁸ Then they thought, "Let's destroy everything!"
    So they burned down all the places where God
        was worshiped.

⁹ We no longer see your miraculous signs.
    All the prophets are gone,
    and no one can tell us when it will end.
¹⁰ How long, O God, will you allow our enemies
        to insult you?
    Will you let them dishonor your name forever?

¹¹ Why do you hold back your strong right hand?
    Unleash your powerful fist and destroy them.

¹² You, O God, are my king from ages past,
    bringing salvation to the earth.
¹³ You split the sea by your strength
    and smashed the heads of the sea monsters.
¹⁴ You crushed the heads of Leviathan
    and let the desert animals eat him.
¹⁵ You caused the springs and streams to gush forth,
    and you dried up rivers that never run dry.
¹⁶ Both day and night belong to you;
    you made the starlight and the sun.
¹⁷ You set the boundaries of the earth,
    and you made both summer and winter.

¹⁸ See how these enemies insult you, LORD.
    A foolish nation has dishonored your name.
¹⁹ Don't let these wild beasts destroy your turtledoves.
    Don't forget your suffering people forever.

²⁰ Remember your covenant promises,
    for the land is full of darkness and violence!
²¹ Don't let the downtrodden be humiliated again.
    Instead, let the poor and needy praise
        your name.

²² Arise, O God, and defend your cause.
    Remember how these fools insult you all day long.
²³ Don't overlook what your enemies have said
    or their growing uproar.

🔥 PSALM 75

For the choir director: A psalm of Asaph. A song to be sung to the tune
"Do Not Destroy!"

¹ We thank you, O God!
    We give thanks because you are near.
    People everywhere tell of your wonderful deeds.

² God says, "At the time I have planned,
    I will bring justice against the wicked.
³ When the earth quakes and its people live in
        turmoil,
    I am the one who keeps its foundations firm.

Interlude

⁴ "I warned the proud, 'Stop your boasting!'
    I told the wicked, 'Don't raise your fists!
⁵ Don't raise your fists in defiance at the heavens
    or speak with such arrogance.'"
⁶ For no one on earth—from east or west,
    or even from the wilderness—
    should raise a defiant fist.

⁷ It is God alone who judges;
   he decides who will rise and who will fall.
⁸ For the LORD holds a cup in his hand
   that is full of foaming wine mixed with spices.
He pours out the wine in judgment,
   and all the wicked must drink it,
   draining it to the dregs.

⁹ But as for me, I will always proclaim what God has
      done;
   I will sing praises to the God of Jacob.
¹⁰ For God says, "I will break the strength of the
      wicked,
   but I will increase the power of the godly."

✳ PROVERBS 15

¹ A gentle answer deflects anger,
   but harsh words make tempers flare.

² The tongue of the wise makes knowledge appealing,
   but the mouth of a fool belches out foolishness.

³ The LORD is watching everywhere,
   keeping his eye on both the evil and the good.

⁴ Gentle words are a tree of life;
   a deceitful tongue crushes the spirit.

⁵ Only a fool despises a parent's discipline;
   whoever learns from correction is wise.

⁶ There is treasure in the house of the godly,
   but the earnings of the wicked bring trouble.

⁷ The lips of the wise give good advice;
   the heart of a fool has none to give.

⁸ The LORD detests the sacrifice of the wicked,
   but he delights in the prayers of the upright.

⁹ The LORD detests the way of the wicked,
   but he loves those who pursue godliness.

¹⁰ Whoever abandons the right path will be severely
      disciplined;
   whoever hates correction will die.

¹¹ Even Death and Destruction hold no secrets from
      the LORD.
   How much more does he know the human heart!

¹² Mockers hate to be corrected,
   so they stay away from the wise.

¹³ A glad heart makes a happy face;
   a broken heart crushes the spirit.

¹⁴ A wise person is hungry for knowledge,
   while the fool feeds on trash.

¹⁵ For the despondent, every day brings trouble;
  for the happy heart, life is a continual feast.

¹⁶ Better to have little, with fear for the LORD,
  than to have great treasure and inner turmoil.

¹⁷ A bowl of vegetables with someone you love
  is better than steak with someone you hate.

¹⁸ A hot-tempered person starts fights;
  a cool-tempered person stops them.

¹⁹ A lazy person's way is blocked with briers,
  but the path of the upright is an open highway.

²⁰ Sensible children bring joy to their father;
  foolish children despise their mother.

²¹ Foolishness brings joy to those with no sense;
  a sensible person stays on the right path.

²² Plans go wrong for lack of advice;
  many advisers bring success.

²³ Everyone enjoys a fitting reply;
  it is wonderful to say the right thing at the
    right time!

²⁴ The path of life leads upward for the wise;
  they leave the grave behind.

²⁵ The LORD tears down the house of the proud,
   but he protects the property of widows.

²⁶ The LORD detests evil plans,
   but he delights in pure words.

²⁷ Greed brings grief to the whole family,
   but those who hate bribes will live.

²⁸ The heart of the godly thinks carefully before
      speaking;
   the mouth of the wicked overflows with evil
      words.

²⁹ The LORD is far from the wicked,
   but he hears the prayers of the righteous.

³⁰ A cheerful look brings joy to the heart;
   good news makes for good health.

³¹ If you listen to constructive criticism,
   you will be at home among the wise.

³² If you reject discipline, you only harm yourself;
   but if you listen to correction, you grow in
      understanding.

³³ Fear of the LORD teaches wisdom;
   humility precedes honor.

❦ PSALM 76

For the choir director: A psalm of Asaph. A song to be accompanied by stringed instruments.

¹ God is honored in Judah;
    his name is great in Israel.
² Jerusalem is where he lives;
    Mount Zion is his home.
³ There he has broken the fiery arrows of the enemy,
    the shields and swords and weapons of war.

Interlude

⁴ You are glorious and more majestic
    than the everlasting mountains.
⁵ Our boldest enemies have been plundered.
    They lie before us in the sleep of death.
    No warrior could lift a hand against us.
⁶ At the blast of your breath, O God of Jacob,
    their horses and chariots lay still.

⁷ No wonder you are greatly feared!
    Who can stand before you when your anger
        explodes?
⁸ From heaven you sentenced your enemies;
    the earth trembled and stood silent before you.

⁹ You stand up to judge those who do evil, O God,
    and to rescue the oppressed of the earth.

Interlude

¹⁰ Human defiance only enhances your glory,
    for you use it as a weapon.

¹¹ Make vows to the LORD your God, and keep them.
    Let everyone bring tribute to the Awesome One.
¹² For he breaks the pride of princes,
    and the kings of the earth fear him.

🔥 PSALM 77

For Jeduthun, the choir director: A psalm of Asaph.

¹ I cry out to God; yes, I shout.
    Oh, that God would listen to me!
² When I was in deep trouble,
    I searched for the Lord.
  All night long I prayed, with hands lifted toward
      heaven,
    but my soul was not comforted.
³ I think of God, and I moan,
    overwhelmed with longing for his help. *Interlude*

⁴ You don't let me sleep.
    I am too distressed even to pray!

⁵ I think of the good old days,
    long since ended,
⁶ when my nights were filled with joyful songs.
    I search my soul and ponder the difference now.
⁷ Has the Lord rejected me forever?
    Will he never again be kind to me?
⁸ Is his unfailing love gone forever?
    Have his promises permanently failed?
⁹ Has God forgotten to be gracious?
    Has he slammed the door on his compassion?
                                                    Interlude

¹⁰ And I said, "This is my fate;
    the Most High has turned his hand against me."
¹¹ But then I recall all you have done, O LORD;
    I remember your wonderful deeds of long ago.
¹² They are constantly in my thoughts.
    I cannot stop thinking about your mighty works.

¹³ O God, your ways are holy.
    Is there any god as mighty as you?
¹⁴ You are the God of great wonders!
    You demonstrate your awesome power among
        the nations.
¹⁵ By your strong arm, you redeemed your people,
    the descendants of Jacob and Joseph.   *Interlude*

¹⁶ When the Red Sea saw you, O God,
   its waters looked and trembled!
   The sea quaked to its very depths.
¹⁷ The clouds poured down rain;
   the thunder rumbled in the sky.
   Your arrows of lightning flashed.
¹⁸ Your thunder roared from the whirlwind;
   the lightning lit up the world!
   The earth trembled and shook.
¹⁹ Your road led through the sea,
   your pathway through the mighty waters—
   a pathway no one knew was there!
²⁰ You led your people along that road like a flock
       of sheep,
   with Moses and Aaron as their shepherds.

❦ PSALM 78

A psalm of Asaph.

¹ O my people, listen to my instructions.
   Open your ears to what I am saying,
²   for I will speak to you in a parable.
 I will teach you hidden lessons from our past—
³   stories we have heard and known,
   stories our ancestors handed down to us.

⁴ We will not hide these truths from our children;
    we will tell the next generation
about the glorious deeds of the LORD,
    about his power and his mighty wonders.
⁵ For he issued his laws to Jacob;
    he gave his instructions to Israel.
He commanded our ancestors
    to teach them to their children,
⁶ so the next generation might know them—
    even the children not yet born—
    and they in turn will teach their own children.
⁷ So each generation should set its hope anew
      on God,
    not forgetting his glorious miracles
    and obeying his commands.
⁸ Then they will not be like their ancestors—
    stubborn, rebellious, and unfaithful,
    refusing to give their hearts to God.

⁹ The warriors of Ephraim, though armed with bows,
    turned their backs and fled on the day of battle.
¹⁰ They did not keep God's covenant
    and refused to live by his instructions.
¹¹ They forgot what he had done—
    the great wonders he had shown them,

¹² the miracles he did for their ancestors
    on the plain of Zoan in the land of Egypt.
¹³ For he divided the sea and led them through,
    making the water stand up like walls!
¹⁴ In the daytime he led them by a cloud,
    and all night by a pillar of fire.
¹⁵ He split open the rocks in the wilderness
    to give them water, as from a gushing spring.
¹⁶ He made streams pour from the rock,
    making the waters flow down like a river!

¹⁷ Yet they kept on sinning against him,
    rebelling against the Most High in the
        desert.
¹⁸ They stubbornly tested God in their hearts,
    demanding the foods they craved.
¹⁹ They even spoke against God himself, saying,
    "God can't give us food in the wilderness.
²⁰ Yes, he can strike a rock so water gushes out,
    but he can't give his people bread and meat."
²¹ When the LORD heard them, he was furious.
    The fire of his wrath burned against Jacob.
    Yes, his anger rose against Israel,
²² for they did not believe God
    or trust him to care for them.

²³ But he commanded the skies to open;
   he opened the doors of heaven.
²⁴ He rained down manna for them to eat;
   he gave them bread from heaven.
²⁵ They ate the food of angels!
   God gave them all they could hold.
²⁶ He released the east wind in the heavens
   and guided the south wind by his mighty
      power.
²⁷ He rained down meat as thick as dust—
   birds as plentiful as the sand on the seashore!
²⁸ He caused the birds to fall within their camp
   and all around their tents.
²⁹ The people ate their fill.
   He gave them what they craved.
³⁰ But before they satisfied their craving,
   while the meat was yet in their mouths,
³¹ the anger of God rose against them,
   and he killed their strongest men.
   He struck down the finest of Israel's young men.

³² But in spite of this, the people kept sinning.
   Despite his wonders, they refused to trust him.
³³ So he ended their lives in failure,
   their years in terror.

³⁴ When God began killing them,
  they finally sought him.
  They repented and took God seriously.
³⁵ Then they remembered that God was their
      rock,
  that God Most High was their redeemer.
³⁶ But all they gave him was lip service;
  they lied to him with their tongues.
³⁷ Their hearts were not loyal to him.
  They did not keep his covenant.
³⁸ Yet he was merciful and forgave their sins
  and did not destroy them all.
Many times he held back his anger
  and did not unleash his fury!
³⁹ For he remembered that they were merely
      mortal,
  gone like a breath of wind that never returns.

⁴⁰ Oh, how often they rebelled against him in the
      wilderness
  and grieved his heart in that dry wasteland.
⁴¹ Again and again they tested God's patience
  and provoked the Holy One of Israel.
⁴² They did not remember his power
  and how he rescued them from their enemies.

⁴³ They did not remember his miraculous
        signs in Egypt,
    his wonders on the plain of Zoan.
⁴⁴ For he turned their rivers into blood,
        so no one could drink from the streams.
⁴⁵ He sent vast swarms of flies to consume them
        and hordes of frogs to ruin them.
⁴⁶ He gave their crops to caterpillars;
        their harvest was consumed by locusts.
⁴⁷ He destroyed their grapevines with hail
        and shattered their sycamore-figs with sleet.
⁴⁸ He abandoned their cattle to the hail,
        their livestock to bolts of lightning.
⁴⁹ He loosed on them his fierce anger—
        all his fury, rage, and hostility.
    He dispatched against them
        a band of destroying angels.
⁵⁰ He turned his anger against them;
        he did not spare the Egyptians' lives
        but ravaged them with the plague.
⁵¹ He killed the oldest son in each Egyptian
        family,
    the flower of youth throughout the land
        of Egypt.

⁵² But he led his own people like a flock of sheep,
  guiding them safely through the wilderness.
⁵³ He kept them safe so they were not afraid;
  but the sea covered their enemies.
⁵⁴ He brought them to the border of his holy land,
  to this land of hills he had won for them.
⁵⁵ He drove out the nations before them;
  he gave them their inheritance by lot.
  He settled the tribes of Israel into their homes.

⁵⁶ But they kept testing and rebelling against God
    Most High.
  They did not obey his laws.
⁵⁷ They turned back and were as faithless as their
    parents.
  They were as undependable as a crooked bow.
⁵⁸ They angered God by building shrines to other gods;
  they made him jealous with their idols.
⁵⁹ When God heard them, he was very angry,
  and he completely rejected Israel.
⁶⁰ Then he abandoned his dwelling at Shiloh,
  the Tabernacle where he had lived among the
    people.
⁶¹ He allowed the Ark of his might to be captured;
  he surrendered his glory into enemy hands.

^{62} He gave his people over to be butchered by the sword,
　　because he was so angry with his own people—
　　　　his special possession.
^{63} Their young men were killed by fire;
　　their young women died before singing their
　　　　wedding songs.
^{64} Their priests were slaughtered,
　　and their widows could not mourn their deaths.

^{65} Then the Lord rose up as though waking from sleep,
　　like a warrior aroused from a drunken stupor.
^{66} He routed his enemies
　　and sent them to eternal shame.
^{67} But he rejected Joseph's descendants;
　　he did not choose the tribe of Ephraim.
^{68} He chose instead the tribe of Judah,
　　and Mount Zion, which he loved.
^{69} There he built his sanctuary as high as the heavens,
　　as solid and enduring as the earth.
^{70} He chose his servant David,
　　calling him from the sheep pens.
^{71} He took David from tending the ewes and lambs
　　and made him the shepherd of Jacob's
　　　　descendants—
　　God's own people, Israel.

⁷² He cared for them with a true heart
  and led them with skillful hands.

❦ PSALM 79
A psalm of Asaph.

¹ O God, pagan nations have conquered your land,
  your special possession.
 They have defiled your holy Temple
  and made Jerusalem a heap of ruins.
² They have left the bodies of your servants
  as food for the birds of heaven.
 The flesh of your godly ones
  has become food for the wild animals.
³ Blood has flowed like water all around Jerusalem;
  no one is left to bury the dead.
⁴ We are mocked by our neighbors,
   an object of scorn and derision to those
    around us.

⁵ O LORD, how long will you be angry with us?
   Forever?
  How long will your jealousy burn like fire?
⁶ Pour out your wrath on the nations that refuse
   to acknowledge you—
  on kingdoms that do not call upon your name.

⁷ For they have devoured your people Israel,
   making the land a desolate wilderness.
⁸ Do not hold us guilty for the sins of our ancestors!
   Let your compassion quickly meet our needs,
   for we are on the brink of despair.

⁹ Help us, O God of our salvation!
   Help us for the glory of your name.
 Save us and forgive our sins
   for the honor of your name.
¹⁰ Why should pagan nations be allowed to scoff,
   asking, "Where is their God?"
 Show us your vengeance against the nations,
   for they have spilled the blood of your servants.
¹¹ Listen to the moaning of the prisoners.
   Demonstrate your great power by saving those
      condemned to die.

¹² O Lord, pay back our neighbors seven times
   for the scorn they have hurled at you.
¹³ Then we your people, the sheep of your pasture,
   will thank you forever and ever,
   praising your greatness from generation to
      generation.

✳ PROVERBS 16

¹ We can make our own plans,
  but the LORD gives the right answer.

² People may be pure in their own eyes,
  but the LORD examines their motives.

³ Commit your actions to the LORD,
  and your plans will succeed.

⁴ The LORD has made everything for his
    own purposes,
  even the wicked for a day of disaster.

⁵ The LORD detests the proud;
  they will surely be punished.

⁶ Unfailing love and faithfulness make atonement
    for sin.
  By fearing the LORD, people avoid evil.

⁷ When people's lives please the LORD,
  even their enemies are at peace with them.

⁸ Better to have little, with godliness,
  than to be rich and dishonest.

⁹ We can make our plans,
  but the LORD determines our steps.

¹⁰ The king speaks with divine wisdom;
    he must never judge unfairly.

¹¹ The LORD demands accurate scales and balances;
    he sets the standards for fairness.

¹² A king detests wrongdoing,
    for his rule is built on justice.

¹³ The king is pleased with words from
        righteous lips;
    he loves those who speak honestly.

¹⁴ The anger of the king is a deadly threat;
    the wise will try to appease it.

¹⁵ When the king smiles, there is life;
    his favor refreshes like a spring rain.

¹⁶ How much better to get wisdom than gold,
    and good judgment than silver!

¹⁷ The path of the virtuous leads away from evil;
    whoever follows that path is safe.

¹⁸ Pride goes before destruction,
    and haughtiness before a fall.

¹⁹ Better to live humbly with the poor
    than to share plunder with the proud.

²⁰ Those who listen to instruction will prosper;
    those who trust the LORD will be joyful.

²¹ The wise are known for their understanding,
    and pleasant words are persuasive.

²² Discretion is a life-giving fountain to those who
       possess it,
    but discipline is wasted on fools.

²³ From a wise mind comes wise speech;
    the words of the wise are persuasive.

²⁴ Kind words are like honey—
    sweet to the soul and healthy for the body.

²⁵ There is a path before each person that seems right,
    but it ends in death.

²⁶ It is good for workers to have an appetite;
    an empty stomach drives them on.

²⁷ Scoundrels create trouble;
    their words are a destructive blaze.

²⁸ A troublemaker plants seeds of strife;
    gossip separates the best of friends.

²⁹ Violent people mislead their companions,
    leading them down a harmful path.

^{30} With narrowed eyes, people plot evil;
   with a smirk, they plan their mischief.

^{31} Gray hair is a crown of glory;
   it is gained by living a godly life.

^{32} Better to be patient than powerful;
   better to have self-control than to conquer
      a city.

^{33} We may throw the dice,
   but the LORD determines how they fall.

DAY SEVENTEEN

🔥 PSALM 80

For the choir director: A psalm of Asaph, to be sung to the tune "Lilies of the Covenant."

¹ Please listen, O Shepherd of Israel,
    you who lead Joseph's descendants like a flock.
  O God, enthroned above the cherubim,
    display your radiant glory
²   to Ephraim, Benjamin, and Manasseh.
  Show us your mighty power.
    Come to rescue us!

³ Turn us again to yourself, O God.
    Make your face shine down upon us.
    Only then will we be saved.
⁴ O LORD God of Heaven's Armies,
    how long will you be angry with our prayers?
⁵ You have fed us with sorrow
    and made us drink tears by the bucketful.
⁶ You have made us the scorn of neighboring nations.
    Our enemies treat us as a joke.

⁷ Turn us again to yourself, O God of Heaven's Armies.
    Make your face shine down upon us.
    Only then will we be saved.

⁸ You brought us from Egypt like a grapevine;
   you drove away the pagan nations and
      transplanted us into your land.
⁹ You cleared the ground for us,
   and we took root and filled the land.
¹⁰ Our shade covered the mountains;
   our branches covered the mighty cedars.
¹¹ We spread our branches west to the
      Mediterranean Sea;
   our shoots spread east to the Euphrates River.
¹² But now, why have you broken down our walls
   so that all who pass by may steal our fruit?
¹³ The wild boar from the forest devours it,
   and the wild animals feed on it.

¹⁴ Come back, we beg you, O God of Heaven's
      Armies.
   Look down from heaven and see our plight.
   Take care of this grapevine
¹⁵   that you yourself have planted,
   this son you have raised for yourself.
¹⁶ For we are chopped up and burned by our enemies.
   May they perish at the sight of your frown.
¹⁷ Strengthen the man you love,
   the son of your choice.

¹⁸ Then we will never abandon you again.

Revive us so we can call on your name once more.

¹⁹ Turn us again to yourself, O LORD God of
Heaven's Armies.

Make your face shine down upon us.

Only then will we be saved.

🌿 PSALM 81

*For the choir director: A psalm of Asaph, to be accompanied by
a stringed instrument.*

¹ Sing praises to God, our strength.

Sing to the God of Jacob.

² Sing! Beat the tambourine.

Play the sweet lyre and the harp.

³ Blow the ram's horn at new moon,

and again at full moon to call a festival!

⁴ For this is required by the decrees of Israel;

it is a regulation of the God of Jacob.

⁵ He made it a law for Israel

when he attacked Egypt to set us free.

I heard an unknown voice say,

⁶ "Now I will take the load from your shoulders;

I will free your hands from their heavy tasks.

⁷ You cried to me in trouble, and I saved you;
  I answered out of the thundercloud
  and tested your faith when there was no water
    at Meribah.   *Interlude*

⁸ "Listen to me, O my people, while I give you stern
    warnings.
  O Israel, if you would only listen to me!
⁹ You must never have a foreign god;
  you must not bow down before a false god.
¹⁰ For it was I, the LORD your God,
  who rescued you from the land of Egypt.
  Open your mouth wide, and I will fill it with
    good things.

¹¹ "But no, my people wouldn't listen.
  Israel did not want me around.
¹² So I let them follow their own stubborn desires,
  living according to their own ideas.
¹³ Oh, that my people would listen to me!
  Oh, that Israel would follow me, walking in
    my paths!
¹⁴ How quickly I would then subdue their enemies!
  How soon my hands would be upon their foes!
¹⁵ Those who hate the LORD would cringe before him;
  they would be doomed forever.

¹⁶ But I would feed you with the finest wheat.
   I would satisfy you with wild honey from
      the rock."

🌿 PSALM 82

A psalm of Asaph.

¹ God presides over heaven's court;
   he pronounces judgment on the heavenly
      beings:
² "How long will you hand down unjust decisions
   by favoring the wicked?   *Interlude*

³ "Give justice to the poor and the orphan;
   uphold the rights of the oppressed and the
      destitute.
⁴ Rescue the poor and helpless;
   deliver them from the grasp of evil people.
⁵ But these oppressors know nothing;
   they are so ignorant!
 They wander about in darkness,
   while the whole world is shaken to the core.
⁶ I say, 'You are gods;
   you are all children of the Most High.
⁷ But you will die like mere mortals
   and fall like every other ruler.'"

⁸ Rise up, O God, and judge the earth,
    for all the nations belong to you.

🕯 PSALM 83

A song. A psalm of Asaph.

¹ O God, do not be silent!
    Do not be deaf.
    Do not be quiet, O God.
² Don't you hear the uproar of your enemies?
    Don't you see that your arrogant enemies are
        rising up?
³ They devise crafty schemes against your people;
    they conspire against your precious ones.
⁴ "Come," they say, "let us wipe out Israel as a nation.
    We will destroy the very memory of its existence."
⁵ Yes, this was their unanimous decision.
    They signed a treaty as allies against you—
⁶ these Edomites and Ishmaelites;
    Moabites and Hagrites;
⁷ Gebalites, Ammonites, and Amalekites;
    and people from Philistia and Tyre.
⁸ Assyria has joined them, too,
    and is allied with the descendants of Lot.

                                        Interlude

⁹ Do to them as you did to the Midianites
and as you did to Sisera and Jabin at the
Kishon River.
¹⁰ They were destroyed at Endor,
and their decaying corpses fertilized the soil.
¹¹ Let their mighty nobles die as Oreb and Zeeb did.
Let all their princes die like Zebah and
Zalmunna,
¹² for they said, "Let us seize for our own use
these pasturelands of God!"
¹³ O my God, scatter them like tumbleweed,
like chaff before the wind!
¹⁴ As a fire burns a forest
and as a flame sets mountains ablaze,
¹⁵ chase them with your fierce storm;
terrify them with your tempest.
¹⁶ Utterly disgrace them
until they submit to your name, O Lord.
¹⁷ Let them be ashamed and terrified forever.
Let them die in disgrace.
¹⁸ Then they will learn that you alone are called the
Lord,
that you alone are the Most High,
supreme over all the earth.

 **PSALM 84**

For the choir director: A psalm of the descendants of Korah, to be accompanied by a stringed instrument.

¹ How lovely is your dwelling place,
O Lord of Heaven's Armies.
² I long, yes, I faint with longing
to enter the courts of the Lord.
With my whole being, body and soul,
I will shout joyfully to the living God.
³ Even the sparrow finds a home,
and the swallow builds her nest and raises her
young
at a place near your altar,
O Lord of Heaven's Armies, my King and my
God!
⁴ What joy for those who can live in your house,
always singing your praises.   *Interlude*

⁵ What joy for those whose strength comes from
the Lord,
who have set their minds on a pilgrimage to
Jerusalem.
⁶ When they walk through the Valley of Weeping,
it will become a place of refreshing springs.
The autumn rains will clothe it with blessings.

⁷ They will continue to grow stronger,
    and each of them will appear before God in
        Jerusalem.

⁸ O Lᴏʀᴅ God of Heaven's Armies, hear my prayer.
    Listen, O God of Jacob.   *Interlude*

⁹ O God, look with favor upon the king, our shield!
    Show favor to the one you have anointed.

¹⁰ A single day in your courts
    is better than a thousand anywhere else!
  I would rather be a gatekeeper in the house of
        my God
    than live the good life in the homes of the wicked.
¹¹ For the Lᴏʀᴅ God is our sun and our shield.
    He gives us grace and glory.
  The Lᴏʀᴅ will withhold no good thing
    from those who do what is right.
¹² O Lᴏʀᴅ of Heaven's Armies,
    what joy for those who trust in you.

❧ PSALM 85

For the choir director: A psalm of the descendants of Korah.

¹ Lᴏʀᴅ, you poured out blessings on your land!
    You restored the fortunes of Israel.

² You forgave the guilt of your people—
    yes, you covered all their sins.   *Interlude*
³ You held back your fury.
    You kept back your blazing anger.

⁴ Now restore us again, O God of our salvation.
    Put aside your anger against us once more.
⁵ Will you be angry with us always?
    Will you prolong your wrath to all generations?
⁶ Won't you revive us again,
    so your people can rejoice in you?
⁷ Show us your unfailing love, O LORD,
    and grant us your salvation.

⁸ I listen carefully to what God the LORD is saying,
    for he speaks peace to his faithful people.
    But let them not return to their foolish ways.
⁹ Surely his salvation is near to those who fear him,
    so our land will be filled with his glory.

¹⁰ Unfailing love and truth have met together.
    Righteousness and peace have kissed!
¹¹ Truth springs up from the earth,
    and righteousness smiles down from heaven.
¹² Yes, the LORD pours down his blessings.
    Our land will yield its bountiful harvest.

¹³ Righteousness goes as a herald before him,
  preparing the way for his steps.

❋ PROVERBS 17

¹ Better a dry crust eaten in peace
  than a house filled with feasting—and conflict.

² A wise servant will rule over the master's disgraceful
    son
  and will share the inheritance of the master's
    children.

³ Fire tests the purity of silver and gold,
  but the LORD tests the heart.

⁴ Wrongdoers eagerly listen to gossip;
  liars pay close attention to slander.

⁵ Those who mock the poor insult their Maker;
  those who rejoice at the misfortune of others
    will be punished.

⁶ Grandchildren are the crowning glory of the aged;
  parents are the pride of their children.

⁷ Eloquent words are not fitting for a fool;
  even less are lies fitting for a ruler.

⁸ A bribe is like a lucky charm;
  whoever gives one will prosper!

⁹ Love prospers when a fault is forgiven,
   but dwelling on it separates close friends.

¹⁰ A single rebuke does more for a person of
      understanding
   than a hundred lashes on the back of a fool.

¹¹ Evil people are eager for rebellion,
   but they will be severely punished.

¹² It is safer to meet a bear robbed of her cubs
   than to confront a fool caught in foolishness.

¹³ If you repay good with evil,
   evil will never leave your house.

¹⁴ Starting a quarrel is like opening a floodgate,
   so stop before a dispute breaks out.

¹⁵ Acquitting the guilty and condemning the innocent—
   both are detestable to the LORD.

¹⁶ It is senseless to pay to educate a fool,
   since he has no heart for learning.

¹⁷ A friend is always loyal,
   and a brother is born to help in time of need.

¹⁸ It's poor judgment to guarantee another person's debt
   or put up security for a friend.

¹⁹ Anyone who loves to quarrel loves sin;
     anyone who trusts in high walls invites disaster.

²⁰ The crooked heart will not prosper;
     the lying tongue tumbles into trouble.

²¹ It is painful to be the parent of a fool;
     there is no joy for the father of a rebel.

²² A cheerful heart is good medicine,
     but a broken spirit saps a person's strength.

²³ The wicked take secret bribes
     to pervert the course of justice.

²⁴ Sensible people keep their eyes glued on wisdom,
     but a fool's eyes wander to the ends of the earth.

²⁵ Foolish children bring grief to their father
     and bitterness to the one who gave them birth.

²⁶ It is wrong to punish the godly for being good
     or to flog leaders for being honest.

²⁷ A truly wise person uses few words;
     a person with understanding is even-tempered.

²⁸ Even fools are thought wise when they keep silent;
     with their mouths shut, they seem intelligent.

🌿 PSALM 86

A prayer of David.

1 Bend down, O LORD, and hear my prayer;
    answer me, for I need your help.

2 Protect me, for I am devoted to you.
    Save me, for I serve you and trust you.
    You are my God.

3 Be merciful to me, O Lord,
    for I am calling on you constantly.

4 Give me happiness, O Lord,
    for I give myself to you.

5 O Lord, you are so good, so ready to
        forgive,
    so full of unfailing love for all who ask
        for your help.

6 Listen closely to my prayer, O LORD;
    hear my urgent cry.

7 I will call to you whenever I'm in trouble,
    and you will answer me.

8 No pagan god is like you, O Lord.
    None can do what you do!

⁹ All the nations you made
   will come and bow before you, Lord;
   they will praise your holy name.
¹⁰ For you are great and perform wonderful deeds.
   You alone are God.

¹¹ Teach me your ways, O LORD,
   that I may live according to your truth!
  Grant me purity of heart,
   so that I may honor you.
¹² With all my heart I will praise you, O Lord my God.
   I will give glory to your name forever,
¹³ for your love for me is very great.
   You have rescued me from the depths of death.

¹⁴ O God, insolent people rise up against me;
   a violent gang is trying to kill me.
   You mean nothing to them.
¹⁵ But you, O Lord,
   are a God of compassion and mercy,
  slow to get angry
   and filled with unfailing love and faithfulness.
¹⁶ Look down and have mercy on me.
   Give your strength to your servant;
   save me, the son of your servant.

¹⁷ Send me a sign of your favor.

　　Then those who hate me will be put to shame,

　　for you, O Lᴏʀᴅ, help and comfort me.

🔥 Psalm 87

A song. A psalm of the descendants of Korah.

¹ On the holy mountain

　　stands the city founded by the Lᴏʀᴅ.

² He loves the city of Jerusalem

　　more than any other city in Israel.

³ O city of God,

　　what glorious things are said of you!　　　*Interlude*

⁴ I will count Egypt and Babylon among those who

　　　　know me—

　　also Philistia and Tyre, and even distant Ethiopia.

　　They have all become citizens of Jerusalem!

⁵ Regarding Jerusalem it will be said,

　　"Everyone enjoys the rights of citizenship there."

　　And the Most High will personally bless this city.

⁶ When the Lᴏʀᴅ registers the nations, he will say,

　　"They have all become citizens of Jerusalem."

　　　　　　　　　　　　　　　　　　　　Interlude

⁷ The people will play flutes and sing,

　　"The source of my life springs from Jerusalem!"

🌿 PSALM 88

For the choir director: A psalm of the descendants of Korah. A song to be sung to the tune "The Suffering of Affliction." A psalm of Heman the Ezrahite.

¹ O LORD, God of my salvation,
    I cry out to you by day.
    I come to you at night.
² Now hear my prayer;
    listen to my cry.
³ For my life is full of troubles,
    and death draws near.
⁴ I am as good as dead,
    like a strong man with no strength left.
⁵ They have left me among the dead,
    and I lie like a corpse in a grave.
  I am forgotten,
    cut off from your care.
⁶ You have thrown me into the lowest pit,
    into the darkest depths.
⁷ Your anger weighs me down;
    with wave after wave you have engulfed me.

                                        Interlude

⁸ You have driven my friends away
    by making me repulsive to them.

I am in a trap with no way of escape.
9   My eyes are blinded by my tears.
Each day I beg for your help, O LORD;
    I lift my hands to you for mercy.
10 Are your wonderful deeds of any use to the dead?
    Do the dead rise up and praise you?   *Interlude*

11 Can those in the grave declare your unfailing love?
    Can they proclaim your faithfulness in the place
        of destruction?
12 Can the darkness speak of your wonderful deeds?
    Can anyone in the land of forgetfulness talk
        about your righteousness?
13 O LORD, I cry out to you.
    I will keep on pleading day by day.
14 O LORD, why do you reject me?
    Why do you turn your face from me?

15 I have been sick and close to death since my youth.
    I stand helpless and desperate before your terrors.
16 Your fierce anger has overwhelmed me.
    Your terrors have paralyzed me.
17 They swirl around me like floodwaters all day long.
    They have engulfed me completely.
18 You have taken away my companions and loved ones.
    Darkness is my closest friend.

🔥 PSALM 89

A psalm of Ethan the Ezrahite.

1 I will sing of the LORD's unfailing love forever!
     Young and old will hear of your faithfulness.
2 Your unfailing love will last forever.
     Your faithfulness is as enduring as the heavens.

3 The LORD said, "I have made a covenant with
          David, my chosen servant.
     I have sworn this oath to him:
4 'I will establish your descendants as kings forever;
     they will sit on your throne from now until
          eternity.'"   *Interlude*
5 All heaven will praise your great wonders, LORD;
     myriads of angels will praise you for your
          faithfulness.
6 For who in all of heaven can compare with the LORD?
     What mightiest angel is anything like the LORD?
7 The highest angelic powers stand in awe of God.
     He is far more awesome than all who surround
          his throne.
8 O LORD God of Heaven's Armies!
     Where is there anyone as mighty as you, O LORD?
     You are entirely faithful.

⁹ You rule the oceans.
  You subdue their storm-tossed waves.
¹⁰ You crushed the great sea monster.
  You scattered your enemies with your mighty arm.
¹¹ The heavens are yours, and the earth is yours;
  everything in the world is yours—you created
    it all.
¹² You created north and south.
  Mount Tabor and Mount Hermon praise your
    name.
¹³ Powerful is your arm!
  Strong is your hand!
  Your right hand is lifted high in glorious strength.
¹⁴ Righteousness and justice are the foundation of
    your throne.
  Unfailing love and truth walk before you as
    attendants.
¹⁵ Happy are those who hear the joyful call to
    worship,
  for they will walk in the light of your presence,
    LORD.
¹⁶ They rejoice all day long in your wonderful
    reputation.
  They exult in your righteousness.

¹⁷ You are their glorious strength.

It pleases you to make us strong.

¹⁸ Yes, our protection comes from the LORD,

and he, the Holy One of Israel, has given us
our king.

¹⁹ Long ago you spoke in a vision to your faithful
people.

You said, "I have raised up a warrior.

I have selected him from the common people
to be king.

²⁰ I have found my servant David.

I have anointed him with my holy oil.

²¹ I will steady him with my hand;

with my powerful arm I will make him strong.

²² His enemies will not defeat him,

nor will the wicked overpower him.

²³ I will beat down his adversaries before him

and destroy those who hate him.

²⁴ My faithfulness and unfailing love will be with him,

and by my authority he will grow in power.

²⁵ I will extend his rule over the sea,

his dominion over the rivers.

²⁶ And he will call out to me, 'You are my Father,

my God, and the Rock of my salvation.'

²⁷ I will make him my firstborn son,
     the mightiest king on earth.
²⁸ I will love him and be kind to him forever;
     my covenant with him will never end.
²⁹ I will preserve an heir for him;
     his throne will be as endless as the days of heaven.
³⁰ But if his descendants forsake my instructions
     and fail to obey my regulations,
³¹ if they do not obey my decrees
     and fail to keep my commands,
³² then I will punish their sin with the rod,
     and their disobedience with beating.
³³ But I will never stop loving him
     nor fail to keep my promise to him.
³⁴ No, I will not break my covenant;
     I will not take back a single word I said.
³⁵ I have sworn an oath to David,
     and in my holiness I cannot lie:
³⁶ His dynasty will go on forever;
     his kingdom will endure as the sun.
³⁷ It will be as eternal as the moon,
     my faithful witness in the sky!"   *Interlude*

³⁸ But now you have rejected him and cast him off.
     You are angry with your anointed king.

³⁹ You have renounced your covenant with him;
    you have thrown his crown in the dust.
⁴⁰ You have broken down the walls protecting him
    and ruined every fort defending him.
⁴¹ Everyone who comes along has robbed him,
    and he has become a joke to his neighbors.
⁴² You have strengthened his enemies
    and made them all rejoice.
⁴³ You have made his sword useless
    and refused to help him in battle.
⁴⁴ You have ended his splendor
    and overturned his throne.
⁴⁵ You have made him old before his time
    and publicly disgraced him.   *Interlude*

⁴⁶ O LORD, how long will this go on?
    Will you hide yourself forever?
    How long will your anger burn like fire?
⁴⁷ Remember how short my life is,
    how empty and futile this human existence!
⁴⁸ No one can live forever; all will die.
    No one can escape the power of the grave.
                                          Interlude

⁴⁹ Lord, where is your unfailing love?
    You promised it to David with a faithful pledge.

[50] Consider, Lord, how your servants are disgraced!
   I carry in my heart the insults of so many people.
[51] Your enemies have mocked me, O LORD;
   they mock your anointed king wherever he goes.

[52] Praise the LORD forever!
   Amen and amen!

BOOK FOUR (PSALMS 90–106)

❧ PSALM 90

A prayer of Moses, the man of God.

[1] Lord, through all the generations
   you have been our home!
[2] Before the mountains were born,
   before you gave birth to the earth and the world,
   from beginning to end, you are God.

[3] You turn people back to dust, saying,
   "Return to dust, you mortals!"
[4] For you, a thousand years are as a passing day,
   as brief as a few night hours.
[5] You sweep people away like dreams that disappear.
   They are like grass that springs up in the morning.
[6] In the morning it blooms and flourishes,
   but by evening it is dry and withered.

⁷ We wither beneath your anger;
    we are overwhelmed by your fury.
⁸ You spread out our sins before you—
    our secret sins—and you see them all.
⁹ We live our lives beneath your wrath,
    ending our years with a groan.

¹⁰ Seventy years are given to us!
    Some even live to eighty.
  But even the best years are filled with pain and
        trouble;
    soon they disappear, and we fly away.
¹¹ Who can comprehend the power of your anger?
    Your wrath is as awesome as the fear you deserve.
¹² Teach us to realize the brevity of life,
    so that we may grow in wisdom.

¹³ O LORD, come back to us!
    How long will you delay?
    Take pity on your servants!
¹⁴ Satisfy us each morning with your unfailing love,
    so we may sing for joy to the end of our lives.
¹⁵ Give us gladness in proportion to our former
        misery!
    Replace the evil years with good.

¹⁶ Let us, your servants, see you work again;
  let our children see your glory.
¹⁷ And may the Lord our God show us his approval
  and make our efforts successful.
  Yes, make our efforts successful!

✳ PROVERBS 18

¹ Unfriendly people care only about themselves;
  they lash out at common sense.

² Fools have no interest in understanding;
  they only want to air their own opinions.

³ Doing wrong leads to disgrace,
  and scandalous behavior brings contempt.

⁴ Wise words are like deep waters;
  wisdom flows from the wise like a bubbling
    brook.

⁵ It is not right to acquit the guilty
  or deny justice to the innocent.

⁶ Fools' words get them into constant quarrels;
  they are asking for a beating.

⁷ The mouths of fools are their ruin;
  they trap themselves with their lips.

⁸ Rumors are dainty morsels
   that sink deep into one's heart.

⁹ A lazy person is as bad as
   someone who destroys things.

¹⁰ The name of the LORD is a strong fortress;
   the godly run to him and are safe.

¹¹ The rich think of their wealth as a strong
       defense;
   they imagine it to be a high wall of safety.

¹² Haughtiness goes before destruction;
   humility precedes honor.

¹³ Spouting off before listening to the facts
   is both shameful and foolish.

¹⁴ The human spirit can endure a sick body,
   but who can bear a crushed spirit?

¹⁵ Intelligent people are always ready to learn.
   Their ears are open for knowledge.

¹⁶ Giving a gift can open doors;
   it gives access to important people!

¹⁷ The first to speak in court sounds right—
   until the cross-examination begins.

¹⁸ Flipping a coin can end arguments;
    it settles disputes between powerful opponents.

¹⁹ An offended friend is harder to win back than a
        fortified city.
    Arguments separate friends like a gate locked
        with bars.

²⁰ Wise words satisfy like a good meal;
    the right words bring satisfaction.

²¹ The tongue can bring death or life;
    those who love to talk will reap the
        consequences.

²² The man who finds a wife finds a treasure,
    and he receives favor from the LORD.

²³ The poor plead for mercy;
    the rich answer with insults.

²⁴ There are "friends" who destroy each other,
    but a real friend sticks closer than a brother.

DAY NINETEEN

❧ PSALM 91

¹ Those who live in the shelter of the Most High
   will find rest in the shadow of the Almighty.
² This I declare about the LORD:
   He alone is my refuge, my place of safety;
      he is my God, and I trust him.
³ For he will rescue you from every trap
   and protect you from deadly disease.
⁴ He will cover you with his feathers.
   He will shelter you with his wings.
   His faithful promises are your armor and
      protection.
⁵ Do not be afraid of the terrors of the night,
   nor the arrow that flies in the day.
⁶ Do not dread the disease that stalks in darkness,
   nor the disaster that strikes at midday.
⁷ Though a thousand fall at your side,
   though ten thousand are dying around you,
   these evils will not touch you.
⁸ Just open your eyes,
   and see how the wicked are punished.

⁹ If you make the LORD your refuge,
　　if you make the Most High your shelter,
¹⁰ no evil will conquer you;
　　no plague will come near your home.
¹¹ For he will order his angels
　　to protect you wherever you go.
¹² They will hold you up with their hands
　　so you won't even hurt your foot on a stone.
¹³ You will trample upon lions and cobras;
　　you will crush fierce lions and serpents under
　　　your feet!

¹⁴ The LORD says, "I will rescue those who love me.
　　I will protect those who trust in my name.
¹⁵ When they call on me, I will answer;
　　I will be with them in trouble.
　　I will rescue and honor them.
¹⁶ I will reward them with a long life
　　and give them my salvation."

✹ PSALM 92

A psalm. A song to be sung on the Sabbath Day.

¹ It is good to give thanks to the LORD,
　　to sing praises to the Most High.

² It is good to proclaim your unfailing love in the
      morning,
   your faithfulness in the evening,
³ accompanied by a ten-stringed instrument, a harp,
   and the melody of a lyre.

⁴ You thrill me, LORD, with all you have done for me!
   I sing for joy because of what you have done.
⁵ O LORD, what great works you do!
   And how deep are your thoughts.
⁶ Only a simpleton would not know,
   and only a fool would not understand this:
⁷ Though the wicked sprout like weeds
   and evildoers flourish,
      they will be destroyed forever.

⁸ But you, O LORD, will be exalted forever.
⁹ Your enemies, LORD, will surely perish;
   all evildoers will be scattered.
¹⁰ But you have made me as strong as a wild ox.
   You have anointed me with the finest oil.
¹¹ My eyes have seen the downfall of my enemies;
   my ears have heard the defeat of my wicked
      opponents.
¹² But the godly will flourish like palm trees
   and grow strong like the cedars of Lebanon.

13 For they are transplanted to the LORD's
     own house.
    They flourish in the courts of our God.
14 Even in old age they will still produce fruit;
    they will remain vital and green.
15 They will declare, "The LORD is just!
    He is my rock!
    There is no evil in him!"

🔥 PSALM 93

1 The LORD is king! He is robed in majesty.
    Indeed, the LORD is robed in majesty and armed
       with strength.
 The world stands firm
    and cannot be shaken.

2 Your throne, O LORD, has stood from time
     immemorial.
    You yourself are from the everlasting past.
3 The floods have risen up, O LORD.
    The floods have roared like thunder;
    the floods have lifted their pounding waves.
4 But mightier than the violent raging of the seas,
    mightier than the breakers on the shore—
    the LORD above is mightier than these!

⁵ Your royal laws cannot be changed.
 Your reign, O Lord, is holy forever and ever.

🔥 PSALM 94

¹ O Lord, the God of vengeance,
 O God of vengeance, let your glorious justice
  shine forth!
² Arise, O Judge of the earth.
 Give the proud what they deserve.
³ How long, O Lord?
 How long will the wicked be allowed to gloat?
⁴ How long will they speak with arrogance?
 How long will these evil people boast?
⁵ They crush your people, Lord,
 hurting those you claim as your own.
⁶ They kill widows and foreigners
 and murder orphans.
⁷ "The Lord isn't looking," they say,
 "and besides, the God of Israel doesn't care."

⁸ Think again, you fools!
 When will you finally catch on?
⁹ Is he deaf—the one who made your ears?
 Is he blind—the one who formed your eyes?
¹⁰ He punishes the nations—won't he also punish you?

He knows everything—doesn't he also know
  what you are doing?
¹¹ The LORD knows people's thoughts;
  he knows they are worthless!

¹² Joyful are those you discipline, LORD,
  those you teach with your instructions.
¹³ You give them relief from troubled times
  until a pit is dug to capture the wicked.
¹⁴ The LORD will not reject his people;
  he will not abandon his special possession.
¹⁵ Judgment will again be founded on justice,
  and those with virtuous hearts will pursue it.

¹⁶ Who will protect me from the wicked?
  Who will stand up for me against evildoers?
¹⁷ Unless the LORD had helped me,
  I would soon have settled in the silence of the
    grave.
¹⁸ I cried out, "I am slipping!"
  but your unfailing love, O LORD, supported me.
¹⁹ When doubts filled my mind,
  your comfort gave me renewed hope and cheer.

²⁰ Can unjust leaders claim that God is on their side—
  leaders whose decrees permit injustice?

21 They gang up against the righteous
     and condemn the innocent to death.
22 But the LORD is my fortress;
     my God is the mighty rock where I hide.
23 God will turn the sins of evil people back
          on them.
     He will destroy them for their sins.
     The LORD our God will destroy them.

❧ PSALM 95

1 Come, let us sing to the LORD!
     Let us shout joyfully to the Rock of our
          salvation.
2 Let us come to him with thanksgiving.
     Let us sing psalms of praise to him.
3 For the LORD is a great God,
     a great King above all gods.
4 He holds in his hands the depths of the earth
     and the mightiest mountains.
5 The sea belongs to him, for he made it.
     His hands formed the dry land, too.

6 Come, let us worship and bow down.
     Let us kneel before the LORD our maker,
7   for he is our God.

We are the people he watches over,
    the flock under his care.

If only you would listen to his voice today!
8 The LORD says, "Don't harden your hearts as Israel
    did at Meribah,
    as they did at Massah in the wilderness.
9 For there your ancestors tested and tried my
    patience,
    even though they saw everything I did.
10 For forty years I was angry with them, and I said,
    'They are a people whose hearts turn away
        from me.
    They refuse to do what I tell them.'
11 So in my anger I took an oath:
    'They will never enter my place of rest.'"

✳ PROVERBS 19

1 Better to be poor and honest
    than to be dishonest and a fool.

2 Enthusiasm without knowledge is no good;
    haste makes mistakes.

3 People ruin their lives by their own foolishness
    and then are angry at the LORD.

4 Wealth makes many "friends";
    poverty drives them all away.

5 A false witness will not go unpunished,
    nor will a liar escape.

6 Many seek favors from a ruler;
    everyone is the friend of a person who
        gives gifts!

7 The relatives of the poor despise them;
    how much more will their friends avoid them!
  Though the poor plead with them,
    their friends are gone.

8 To acquire wisdom is to love yourself;
    people who cherish understanding will prosper.

9 A false witness will not go unpunished,
    and a liar will be destroyed.

10 It isn't right for a fool to live in luxury
    or for a slave to rule over princes!

11 Sensible people control their temper;
    they earn respect by overlooking wrongs.

12 The king's anger is like a lion's roar,
    but his favor is like dew on the grass.

¹³ A foolish child is a calamity to a father;
  a quarrelsome wife is as annoying as constant
    dripping.

¹⁴ Fathers can give their sons an inheritance of houses
    and wealth,
  but only the LORD can give an understanding
    wife.

¹⁵ Lazy people sleep soundly,
  but idleness leaves them hungry.

¹⁶ Keep the commandments and keep your life;
  despising them leads to death.

¹⁷ If you help the poor, you are lending to the LORD—
  and he will repay you!

¹⁸ Discipline your children while there is hope.
  Otherwise you will ruin their lives.

¹⁹ Hot-tempered people must pay the penalty.
  If you rescue them once, you will have to do
    it again.

²⁰ Get all the advice and instruction you can,
  so you will be wise the rest of your life.

²¹ You can make many plans,
  but the LORD's purpose will prevail.

²² Loyalty makes a person attractive.
　　It is better to be poor than dishonest.

²³ Fear of the LORD leads to life,
　　bringing security and protection from harm.

²⁴ Lazy people take food in their hand
　　but don't even lift it to their mouth.

²⁵ If you punish a mocker, the simpleminded will
　　　learn a lesson;
　　if you correct the wise, they will be all the wiser.

²⁶ Children who mistreat their father or chase away
　　　their mother
　　are an embarrassment and a public disgrace.

²⁷ If you stop listening to instruction, my child,
　　you will turn your back on knowledge.

²⁸ A corrupt witness makes a mockery of justice;
　　the mouth of the wicked gulps down evil.

²⁹ Punishment is made for mockers,
　　and the backs of fools are made to be beaten.

🔥 PSALM 96

¹ Sing a new song to the LORD!
  Let the whole earth sing to the LORD!
² Sing to the LORD; praise his name.
  Each day proclaim the good news that he saves.
³ Publish his glorious deeds among the nations.
  Tell everyone about the amazing things he does.
⁴ Great is the LORD! He is most worthy of praise!
  He is to be feared above all gods.
⁵ The gods of other nations are mere idols,
  but the LORD made the heavens!
⁶ Honor and majesty surround him;
  strength and beauty fill his sanctuary.

⁷ O nations of the world, recognize the LORD;
  recognize that the LORD is glorious and strong.
⁸ Give to the LORD the glory he deserves!
  Bring your offering and come into his courts.
⁹ Worship the LORD in all his holy splendor.
  Let all the earth tremble before him.
¹⁰ Tell all the nations, "The LORD reigns!"
  The world stands firm and cannot be shaken.
  He will judge all peoples fairly.

¹¹ Let the heavens be glad, and the earth rejoice!
　　Let the sea and everything in it shout
　　　his praise!
¹² Let the fields and their crops burst out
　　　with joy!
　　Let the trees of the forest sing for joy
¹³ before the Lord, for he is coming!
　　He is coming to judge the earth.
　He will judge the world with justice,
　　and the nations with his truth.

❧ PSALM 97

¹ The Lord is king!
　　Let the earth rejoice!
　　Let the farthest coastlands be glad.
² Dark clouds surround him.
　　Righteousness and justice are the foundation
　　　of his throne.
³ Fire spreads ahead of him
　　and burns up all his foes.
⁴ His lightning flashes out across the world.
　　The earth sees and trembles.
⁵ The mountains melt like wax before the Lord,
　　before the Lord of all the earth.

⁶ The heavens proclaim his righteousness;
     every nation sees his glory.
⁷ Those who worship idols are disgraced—
     all who brag about their worthless gods—
     for every god must bow to him.
⁸ Jerusalem has heard and rejoiced,
     and all the towns of Judah are glad
     because of your justice, O LORD!
⁹ For you, O LORD, are supreme over all the earth;
     you are exalted far above all gods.

¹⁰ You who love the LORD, hate evil!
     He protects the lives of his godly people
     and rescues them from the power of the wicked.
¹¹ Light shines on the godly,
     and joy on those whose hearts are right.
¹² May all who are godly rejoice in the LORD
     and praise his holy name!

❧ PSALM 98
A psalm.

¹ Sing a new song to the LORD,
     for he has done wonderful deeds.
   His right hand has won a mighty victory;
     his holy arm has shown his saving power!

² The LORD has announced his victory
and has revealed his righteousness to every nation!
³ He has remembered his promise to love and be
faithful to Israel.
The ends of the earth have seen the victory
of our God.

⁴ Shout to the LORD, all the earth;
break out in praise and sing for joy!
⁵ Sing your praise to the LORD with the harp,
with the harp and melodious song,
⁶ with trumpets and the sound of the ram's horn.
Make a joyful symphony before the LORD, the King!

⁷ Let the sea and everything in it shout his praise!
Let the earth and all living things join in.
⁸ Let the rivers clap their hands in glee!
Let the hills sing out their songs of joy
⁹ before the LORD,
for he is coming to judge the earth.
He will judge the world with justice,
and the nations with fairness.

❦ PSALM 99

¹ The LORD is king!
Let the nations tremble!

He sits on his throne between the cherubim.
    Let the whole earth quake!
² The LORD sits in majesty in Jerusalem,
    exalted above all the nations.
³ Let them praise your great and awesome name.
    Your name is holy!
⁴ Mighty King, lover of justice,
    you have established fairness.
You have acted with justice
    and righteousness throughout Israel.
⁵ Exalt the LORD our God!
    Bow low before his feet, for he is holy!

⁶ Moses and Aaron were among his priests;
    Samuel also called on his name.
They cried to the LORD for help,
    and he answered them.
⁷ He spoke to Israel from the pillar of cloud,
    and they followed the laws and decrees he gave
        them.
⁸ O LORD our God, you answered them.
    You were a forgiving God to them,
    but you punished them when they went
        wrong.

⁹ Exalt the LORD our God,
>   and worship at his holy mountain in Jerusalem,
>   for the LORD our God is holy!

❦ PSALM 100

A psalm of thanksgiving.

¹ Shout with joy to the LORD, all the earth!
²   Worship the LORD with gladness.
>   Come before him, singing with joy.
³ Acknowledge that the LORD is God!
>   He made us, and we are his.
>   We are his people, the sheep of his pasture.
⁴ Enter his gates with thanksgiving;
>   go into his courts with praise.
>   Give thanks to him and praise his name.
⁵ For the LORD is good.
>   His unfailing love continues forever,
>   and his faithfulness continues to each generation.

✳ PROVERBS 20

¹ Wine produces mockers; alcohol leads to brawls.
>   Those led astray by drink cannot be wise.

² The king's fury is like a lion's roar;
>   to rouse his anger is to risk your life.

³ Avoiding a fight is a mark of honor;
   only fools insist on quarreling.

⁴ Those too lazy to plow in the right season
   will have no food at the harvest.

⁵ Though good advice lies deep within the heart,
   a person with understanding will draw it out.

⁶ Many will say they are loyal friends,
   but who can find one who is truly reliable?

⁷ The godly walk with integrity;
   blessed are their children who follow them.

⁸ When a king sits in judgment, he weighs all the
      evidence,
   distinguishing the bad from the good.

⁹ Who can say, "I have cleansed my heart;
   I am pure and free from sin"?

¹⁰ False weights and unequal measures—
   the LORD detests double standards of
      every kind.

¹¹ Even children are known by the way they act,
   whether their conduct is pure, and whether it
      is right.

¹² Ears to hear and eyes to see—
  both are gifts from the LORD.

¹³ If you love sleep, you will end in poverty.
  Keep your eyes open, and there will be plenty
    to eat!

¹⁴ The buyer haggles over the price, saying, "It's
    worthless,"
  then brags about getting a bargain!

¹⁵ Wise words are more valuable
  than much gold and many rubies.

¹⁶ Get security from someone who guarantees a
    stranger's debt.
  Get a deposit if he does it for foreigners.

¹⁷ Stolen bread tastes sweet,
  but it turns to gravel in the mouth.

¹⁸ Plans succeed through good counsel;
  don't go to war without wise advice.

¹⁹ A gossip goes around telling secrets,
  so don't hang around with chatterers.

²⁰ If you insult your father or mother,
  your light will be snuffed out in total darkness.

²¹ An inheritance obtained too early in life
is not a blessing in the end.

²² Don't say, "I will get even for this wrong."
Wait for the Lᴏʀᴅ to handle the matter.

²³ The Lᴏʀᴅ detests double standards;
he is not pleased by dishonest scales.

²⁴ The Lᴏʀᴅ directs our steps,
so why try to understand everything along the way?

²⁵ Don't trap yourself by making a rash promise to God
and only later counting the cost.

²⁶ A wise king scatters the wicked like wheat,
then runs his threshing wheel over them.

²⁷ The Lᴏʀᴅ's light penetrates the human spirit,
exposing every hidden motive.

²⁸ Unfailing love and faithfulness protect the king;
his throne is made secure through love.

²⁹ The glory of the young is their strength;
the gray hair of experience is the splendor
of the old.

³⁰ Physical punishment cleanses away evil;
such discipline purifies the heart.

DAY TWENTY-ONE

🔥 **PSALM 101**

A psalm of David.

¹ I will sing of your love and justice, LORD.
    I will praise you with songs.
² I will be careful to live a blameless life—
    when will you come to help me?
  I will lead a life of integrity
    in my own home.
³ I will refuse to look at
    anything vile and vulgar.
  I hate all who deal crookedly;
    I will have nothing to do with them.
⁴ I will reject perverse ideas
    and stay away from every evil.
⁵ I will not tolerate people who slander their
        neighbors.
    I will not endure conceit and pride.

⁶ I will search for faithful people
    to be my companions.
  Only those who are above reproach
    will be allowed to serve me.

⁷ I will not allow deceivers to serve in my house,
   and liars will not stay in my presence.
⁸ My daily task will be to ferret out the wicked
   and free the city of the LORD from their grip.

🌱 PSALM 102

A prayer of one overwhelmed with trouble, pouring out problems before the LORD.

¹ LORD, hear my prayer!
   Listen to my plea!
² Don't turn away from me
   in my time of distress.
 Bend down to listen,
   and answer me quickly when I call to you.
³ For my days disappear like smoke,
   and my bones burn like red-hot coals.
⁴ My heart is sick, withered like grass,
   and I have lost my appetite.
⁵ Because of my groaning,
   I am reduced to skin and bones.
⁶ I am like an owl in the desert,
   like a little owl in a far-off wilderness.
⁷ I lie awake,
   lonely as a solitary bird on the roof.

⁸ My enemies taunt me day after day.
    They mock and curse me.
⁹ I eat ashes for food.
    My tears run down into my drink
¹⁰ because of your anger and wrath.
    For you have picked me up and thrown
       me out.
¹¹ My life passes as swiftly as the evening shadows.
    I am withering away like grass.

¹² But you, O LORD, will sit on your throne forever.
    Your fame will endure to every generation.
¹³ You will arise and have mercy on Jerusalem—
    and now is the time to pity her,
    now is the time you promised to help.
¹⁴ For your people love every stone in her walls
    and cherish even the dust in her streets.
¹⁵ Then the nations will tremble before the LORD.
    The kings of the earth will tremble before his
       glory.
¹⁶ For the LORD will rebuild Jerusalem.
    He will appear in his glory.
¹⁷ He will listen to the prayers of the destitute.
    He will not reject their pleas.

¹⁸ Let this be recorded for future generations,
    so that a people not yet born will praise the LORD.
¹⁹ Tell them the LORD looked down
    from his heavenly sanctuary.
  He looked down to earth from heaven
²⁰   to hear the groans of the prisoners,
    to release those condemned to die.
²¹ And so the LORD's fame will be celebrated
        in Zion,
    his praises in Jerusalem,
²² when multitudes gather together
    and kingdoms come to worship the LORD.

²³ He broke my strength in midlife,
    cutting short my days.
²⁴ But I cried to him, "O my God, who lives forever,
    don't take my life while I am so young!
²⁵ Long ago you laid the foundation of the earth
    and made the heavens with your hands.
²⁶ They will perish, but you remain forever;
    they will wear out like old clothing.
  You will change them like a garment
    and discard them.
²⁷ But you are always the same;
    you will live forever.

DAY 21   PSALM 102

²⁸ The children of your people
	will live in security.
  Their children's children
	will thrive in your presence."

🕯 PSALM 103

A psalm of David.

¹ Let all that I am praise the LORD;
	with my whole heart, I will praise his holy name.
² Let all that I am praise the LORD;
	may I never forget the good things he does for me.
³ He forgives all my sins
	and heals all my diseases.
⁴ He redeems me from death
	and crowns me with love and tender mercies.
⁵ He fills my life with good things.
	My youth is renewed like the eagle's!

⁶ The LORD gives righteousness
	and justice to all who are treated unfairly.

⁷ He revealed his character to Moses
	and his deeds to the people of Israel.
⁸ The LORD is compassionate and merciful,
	slow to get angry and filled with unfailing love.

⁹ He will not constantly accuse us,
  nor remain angry forever.
¹⁰ He does not punish us for all our sins;
  he does not deal harshly with us, as we deserve.
¹¹ For his unfailing love toward those who fear him
  is as great as the height of the heavens above
    the earth.
¹² He has removed our sins as far from us
  as the east is from the west.
¹³ The LORD is like a father to his children,
  tender and compassionate to those who fear him.
¹⁴ For he knows how weak we are;
  he remembers we are only dust.
¹⁵ Our days on earth are like grass;
  like wildflowers, we bloom and die.
¹⁶ The wind blows, and we are gone—
  as though we had never been here.
¹⁷ But the love of the LORD remains forever
  with those who fear him.
  His salvation extends to the children's children
¹⁸   of those who are faithful to his covenant,
    of those who obey his commandments!

¹⁹ The LORD has made the heavens his throne;
  from there he rules over everything.

20 Praise the LORD, you angels,
  you mighty ones who carry out his plans,
  listening for each of his commands.
21 Yes, praise the LORD, you armies of angels
  who serve him and do his will!
22 Praise the LORD, everything he has created,
  everything in all his kingdom.

  Let all that I am praise the LORD.

✳ PROVERBS 21

1 The king's heart is like a stream of water directed
    by the LORD;
  he guides it wherever he pleases.

2 People may be right in their own eyes,
  but the LORD examines their heart.

3 The LORD is more pleased when we do what is right
    and just
  than when we offer him sacrifices.

4 Haughty eyes, a proud heart,
  and evil actions are all sin.

5 Good planning and hard work lead to prosperity,
  but hasty shortcuts lead to poverty.

⁶ Wealth created by a lying tongue
    is a vanishing mist and a deadly trap.

⁷ The violence of the wicked sweeps them away,
    because they refuse to do what is just.

⁸ The guilty walk a crooked path;
    the innocent travel a straight road.

⁹ It's better to live alone in the corner of an attic
    than with a quarrelsome wife in a lovely home.

¹⁰ Evil people desire evil;
    their neighbors get no mercy from them.

¹¹ If you punish a mocker, the simpleminded become
      wise;
    if you instruct the wise, they will be all
      the wiser.

¹² The Righteous One knows what is going on in the
      homes of the wicked;
    he will bring disaster on them.

¹³ Those who shut their ears to the cries of the poor
    will be ignored in their own time of need.

¹⁴ A secret gift calms anger;
    a bribe under the table pacifies fury.

¹⁵ Justice is a joy to the godly,
    but it terrifies evildoers.

¹⁶ The person who strays from common sense
    will end up in the company of the dead.

¹⁷ Those who love pleasure become poor;
    those who love wine and luxury will never
        be rich.

¹⁸ The wicked are punished in place of the godly,
    and traitors in place of the honest.

¹⁹ It's better to live alone in the desert
    than with a quarrelsome, complaining wife.

²⁰ The wise have wealth and luxury,
    but fools spend whatever they get.

²¹ Whoever pursues righteousness and unfailing love
    will find life, righteousness, and honor.

²² The wise conquer the city of the strong
    and level the fortress in which they trust.

²³ Watch your tongue and keep your mouth shut,
    and you will stay out of trouble.

²⁴ Mockers are proud and haughty;
    they act with boundless arrogance.

²⁵ Despite their desires, the lazy will come to ruin,
　　for their hands refuse to work.

²⁶ Some people are always greedy for more,
　　but the godly love to give!

²⁷ The sacrifice of an evil person is detestable,
　　especially when it is offered with wrong motives.

²⁸ A false witness will be cut off,
　　but a credible witness will be allowed to speak.

²⁹ The wicked bluff their way through,
　　but the virtuous think before they act.

³⁰ No human wisdom or understanding or plan
　　can stand against the LORD.

³¹ The horse is prepared for the day of battle,
　　but the victory belongs to the LORD.

DAY TWENTY-TWO

❦ PSALM 104

¹ Let all that I am praise the LORD.

O LORD my God, how great you are!
　　You are robed with honor and majesty.
²　　You are dressed in a robe of light.
You stretch out the starry curtain of the heavens;
³　　you lay out the rafters of your home in the rain
　　　　clouds.
You make the clouds your chariot;
　　you ride upon the wings of the wind.
⁴ The winds are your messengers;
　　flames of fire are your servants.

⁵ You placed the world on its foundation
　　so it would never be moved.
⁶ You clothed the earth with floods of water,
　　water that covered even the mountains.
⁷ At your command, the water fled;
　　at the sound of your thunder, it hurried away.
⁸ Mountains rose and valleys sank
　　to the levels you decreed.
⁹ Then you set a firm boundary for the seas,
　　so they would never again cover the earth.

¹⁰ You make springs pour water into the ravines,
　　 so streams gush down from the mountains.
¹¹ They provide water for all the animals,
　　 and the wild donkeys quench their thirst.
¹² The birds nest beside the streams
　　 and sing among the branches of the trees.
¹³ You send rain on the mountains from your heavenly
　　　　 home,
　　 and you fill the earth with the fruit of
　　　　 your labor.
¹⁴ You cause grass to grow for the livestock
　　 and plants for people to use.
　 You allow them to produce food from the earth—
¹⁵　 wine to make them glad,
　 olive oil to soothe their skin,
　　 and bread to give them strength.
¹⁶ The trees of the LORD are well cared for—
　　 the cedars of Lebanon that he planted.
¹⁷ There the birds make their nests,
　　 and the storks make their homes in the cypresses.
¹⁸ High in the mountains live the wild goats,
　　 and the rocks form a refuge for the hyraxes.

¹⁹ You made the moon to mark the seasons,
　　 and the sun knows when to set.

²⁰ You send the darkness, and it becomes night,
  when all the forest animals prowl about.
²¹ Then the young lions roar for their prey,
  stalking the food provided by God.
²² At dawn they slink back
  into their dens to rest.
²³ Then people go off to their work,
  where they labor until evening.

²⁴ O Lᴏʀᴅ, what a variety of things you have made!
  In wisdom you have made them all.
  The earth is full of your creatures.
²⁵ Here is the ocean, vast and wide,
  teeming with life of every kind,
  both large and small.
²⁶ See the ships sailing along,
  and Leviathan, which you made to play in the sea.

²⁷ They all depend on you
  to give them food as they need it.
²⁸ When you supply it, they gather it.
  You open your hand to feed them,
  and they are richly satisfied.
²⁹ But if you turn away from them, they panic.
  When you take away their breath,
  they die and turn again to dust.

³⁰ When you give them your breath, life is created,
   and you renew the face of the earth.

³¹ May the glory of the LORD continue forever!
   The LORD takes pleasure in all he has made!
³² The earth trembles at his glance;
   the mountains smoke at his touch.

³³ I will sing to the LORD as long as I live.
   I will praise my God to my last breath!
³⁴ May all my thoughts be pleasing to him,
   for I rejoice in the LORD.
³⁵ Let all sinners vanish from the face of the earth;
   let the wicked disappear forever.

Let all that I am praise the LORD.

Praise the LORD!

🌿 PSALM 105

¹ Give thanks to the LORD and proclaim his
      greatness.
   Let the whole world know what he has done.
² Sing to him; yes, sing his praises.
   Tell everyone about his wonderful deeds.
³ Exult in his holy name;
   rejoice, you who worship the LORD.

4 Search for the LORD and for his strength;
     continually seek him.
5 Remember the wonders he has performed,
     his miracles, and the rulings he has given,
6 you children of his servant Abraham,
     you descendants of Jacob, his chosen ones.

7 He is the LORD our God.
     His justice is seen throughout the land.
8 He always stands by his covenant—
     the commitment he made to a thousand
          generations.
9 This is the covenant he made with Abraham
     and the oath he swore to Isaac.
10 He confirmed it to Jacob as a decree,
     and to the people of Israel as a never-ending
          covenant:
11 "I will give you the land of Canaan
     as your special possession."

12 He said this when they were few in number,
     a tiny group of strangers in Canaan.
13 They wandered from nation to nation,
     from one kingdom to another.
14 Yet he did not let anyone oppress them.
     He warned kings on their behalf:

¹⁵ "Do not touch my chosen people,
  and do not hurt my prophets."

¹⁶ He called for a famine on the land of Canaan,
  cutting off its food supply.
¹⁷ Then he sent someone to Egypt ahead of them—
  Joseph, who was sold as a slave.
¹⁸ They bruised his feet with fetters
  and placed his neck in an iron collar.
¹⁹ Until the time came to fulfill his dreams,
  the LORD tested Joseph's character.
²⁰ Then Pharaoh sent for him and set him free;
  the ruler of the nation opened his prison door.
²¹ Joseph was put in charge of all the king's
    household;
  he became ruler over all the king's possessions.
²² He could instruct the king's aides as he pleased
  and teach the king's advisers.

²³ Then Israel arrived in Egypt;
  Jacob lived as a foreigner in the land of Ham.
²⁴ And the LORD multiplied the people of Israel
  until they became too mighty for their enemies.
²⁵ Then he turned the Egyptians against the Israelites,
  and they plotted against the LORD's servants.

²⁶ But the Lord sent his servant Moses,
along with Aaron, whom he had chosen.
²⁷ They performed miraculous signs among the
Egyptians,
and wonders in the land of Ham.
²⁸ The Lord blanketed Egypt in darkness,
for they had defied his commands to let his
people go.
²⁹ He turned their water into blood,
poisoning all the fish.
³⁰ Then frogs overran the land
and even invaded the king's bedrooms.
³¹ When the Lord spoke, flies descended on the
Egyptians,
and gnats swarmed across Egypt.
³² He sent them hail instead of rain,
and lightning flashed over the land.
³³ He ruined their grapevines and fig trees
and shattered all the trees.
³⁴ He spoke, and hordes of locusts came—
young locusts beyond number.
³⁵ They ate up everything green in the land,
destroying all the crops in their fields.

³⁶ Then he killed the oldest son in each Egyptian home,
  the pride and joy of each family.

³⁷ The LORD brought his people out of Egypt, loaded
  with silver and gold;
  and not one among the tribes of Israel even
  stumbled.

³⁸ Egypt was glad when they were gone,
  for they feared them greatly.

³⁹ The LORD spread a cloud above them as a covering
  and gave them a great fire to light the darkness.

⁴⁰ They asked for meat, and he sent them quail;
  he satisfied their hunger with manna—bread
  from heaven.

⁴¹ He split open a rock, and water gushed out
  to form a river through the dry wasteland.

⁴² For he remembered his sacred promise
  to his servant Abraham.

⁴³ So he brought his people out of Egypt with joy,
  his chosen ones with rejoicing.

⁴⁴ He gave his people the lands of pagan nations,
  and they harvested crops that others had planted.

⁴⁵ All this happened so they would follow his decrees
  and obey his instructions.

  Praise the LORD!

✳ PROVERBS 22

1 Choose a good reputation over great riches;
   being held in high esteem is better than silver
      or gold.

2 The rich and poor have this in common:
   The LORD made them both.

3 A prudent person foresees danger and takes
      precautions.
   The simpleton goes blindly on and suffers
      the consequences.

4 True humility and fear of the LORD
   lead to riches, honor, and long life.

5 Corrupt people walk a thorny, treacherous road;
   whoever values life will avoid it.

6 Direct your children onto the right path,
   and when they are older, they will not leave it.

7 Just as the rich rule the poor,
   so the borrower is servant to the lender.

8 Those who plant injustice will harvest disaster,
   and their reign of terror will come to an end.

9 Blessed are those who are generous,
   because they feed the poor.

¹⁰ Throw out the mocker, and fighting goes, too.
   Quarrels and insults will disappear.

¹¹ Whoever loves a pure heart and gracious speech
   will have the king as a friend.

¹² The LORD preserves those with knowledge,
   but he ruins the plans of the treacherous.

¹³ The lazy person claims, "There's a lion out there!
   If I go outside, I might be killed!"

¹⁴ The mouth of an immoral woman is a dangerous
      trap;
   those who make the LORD angry will fall into it.

¹⁵ A youngster's heart is filled with foolishness,
   but physical discipline will drive it far away.

¹⁶ A person who gets ahead by oppressing the poor
   or by showering gifts on the rich will end in
      poverty.

¹⁷ Listen to the words of the wise;
   apply your heart to my instruction.
¹⁸ For it is good to keep these sayings in your heart
   and always ready on your lips.
¹⁹ I am teaching you today—yes, you—
   so you will trust in the LORD.

²⁰ I have written thirty sayings for you,
   filled with advice and knowledge.
²¹ In this way, you may know the truth
   and take an accurate report to those who sent you.

²² Don't rob the poor just because you can,
   or exploit the needy in court.
²³ For the LORD is their defender.
   He will ruin anyone who ruins them.

²⁴ Don't befriend angry people
   or associate with hot-tempered people,
²⁵ or you will learn to be like them
   and endanger your soul.

²⁶ Don't agree to guarantee another person's debt
   or put up security for someone else.
²⁷ If you can't pay it,
   even your bed will be snatched from under you.

²⁸ Don't cheat your neighbor by moving the ancient
      boundary markers
   set up by previous generations.

²⁹ Do you see any truly competent workers?
   They will serve kings
   rather than working for ordinary people.

🌱 PSALM 106

¹ Praise the LORD!

Give thanks to the LORD, for he is good!
His faithful love endures forever.
² Who can list the glorious miracles of the LORD?
Who can ever praise him enough?
³ There is joy for those who deal justly with others
and always do what is right.

⁴ Remember me, LORD, when you show favor to your
people;
come near and rescue me.
⁵ Let me share in the prosperity of your chosen ones.
Let me rejoice in the joy of your people;
let me praise you with those who are your heritage.

⁶ Like our ancestors, we have sinned.
We have done wrong! We have acted wickedly!
⁷ Our ancestors in Egypt
were not impressed by the LORD's miraculous
deeds.
They soon forgot his many acts of kindness to them.
Instead, they rebelled against him at the Red Sea.

⁸ Even so, he saved them—
    to defend the honor of his name
    and to demonstrate his mighty power.
⁹ He commanded the Red Sea to dry up.
    He led Israel across the sea as if it were a desert.
¹⁰ So he rescued them from their enemies
    and redeemed them from their foes.
¹¹ Then the water returned and covered their enemies;
    not one of them survived.
¹² Then his people believed his promises.
    Then they sang his praise.

¹³ Yet how quickly they forgot what he had done!
    They wouldn't wait for his counsel!
¹⁴ In the wilderness their desires ran wild,
    testing God's patience in that dry wasteland.
¹⁵ So he gave them what they asked for,
    but he sent a plague along with it.
¹⁶ The people in the camp were jealous of Moses
    and envious of Aaron, the LORD's holy priest.
¹⁷ Because of this, the earth opened up;
    it swallowed Dathan
    and buried Abiram and the other rebels.
¹⁸ Fire fell upon their followers;
    a flame consumed the wicked.

¹⁹ The people made a calf at Mount Sinai;
   they bowed before an image made of gold.
²⁰ They traded their glorious God
   for a statue of a grass-eating bull.
²¹ They forgot God, their savior,
   who had done such great things in
      Egypt—
²² such wonderful things in the land of Ham,
   such awesome deeds at the Red Sea.
²³ So he declared he would destroy them.
   But Moses, his chosen one, stepped between
      the Lord and the people.
   He begged him to turn from his anger and not
      destroy them.

²⁴ The people refused to enter the pleasant land,
   for they wouldn't believe his promise to care
      for them.
²⁵ Instead, they grumbled in their tents
   and refused to obey the Lord.
²⁶ Therefore, he solemnly swore
   that he would kill them in the wilderness,
²⁷ that he would scatter their descendants among
      the nations,
   exiling them to distant lands.

²⁸ Then our ancestors joined in the worship
        of Baal at Peor;
    they even ate sacrifices offered to the dead!
²⁹ They angered the LORD with all these things,
    so a plague broke out among them.
³⁰ But Phinehas had the courage to intervene,
    and the plague was stopped.
³¹ So he has been regarded as a righteous man
    ever since that time.

³² At Meribah, too, they angered the LORD,
    causing Moses serious trouble.
³³ They made Moses angry,
    and he spoke foolishly.

³⁴ Israel failed to destroy the nations in the land,
    as the LORD had commanded them.
³⁵ Instead, they mingled among the pagans
    and adopted their evil customs.
³⁶ They worshiped their idols,
    which led to their downfall.
³⁷ They even sacrificed their sons
    and their daughters to the demons.
³⁸ They shed innocent blood,
        the blood of their sons and daughters.

By sacrificing them to the idols of Canaan,
  they polluted the land with murder.
³⁹ They defiled themselves by their evil deeds,
  and their love of idols was adultery in the
    LORD's sight.

⁴⁰ That is why the LORD's anger burned against
    his people,
  and he abhorred his own special possession.
⁴¹ He handed them over to pagan nations,
  and they were ruled by those who hated them.
⁴² Their enemies crushed them
  and brought them under their cruel power.
⁴³ Again and again he rescued them,
  but they chose to rebel against him,
  and they were finally destroyed by their sin.
⁴⁴ Even so, he pitied them in their distress
  and listened to their cries.
⁴⁵ He remembered his covenant with them
  and relented because of his unfailing love.
⁴⁶ He even caused their captors
  to treat them with kindness.

⁴⁷ Save us, O LORD our God!
  Gather us back from among the nations,

so we can thank your holy name
  and rejoice and praise you.

⁴⁸ Praise the LORD, the God of Israel,
  who lives from everlasting to everlasting!
Let all the people say, "Amen!"

Praise the LORD!

BOOK FIVE (PSALMS 107–150)

🔥 P S A L M 1 0 7

¹ Give thanks to the LORD, for he is good!
  His faithful love endures forever.
² Has the LORD redeemed you? Then speak out!
  Tell others he has redeemed you from your
    enemies.
³ For he has gathered the exiles from many lands,
  from east and west,
  from north and south.

⁴ Some wandered in the wilderness,
  lost and homeless.
⁵ Hungry and thirsty,
  they nearly died.
⁶ "LORD, help!" they cried in their trouble,
  and he rescued them from their distress.

7 He led them straight to safety,
   to a city where they could live.
8 Let them praise the Lord for his great love
   and for the wonderful things he has done for
      them.
9 For he satisfies the thirsty
   and fills the hungry with good things.

10 Some sat in darkness and deepest gloom,
   imprisoned in iron chains of misery.
11 They rebelled against the words of God,
   scorning the counsel of the Most High.
12 That is why he broke them with hard labor;
   they fell, and no one was there to help them.
13 "Lord, help!" they cried in their trouble,
   and he saved them from their distress.
14 He led them from the darkness and deepest gloom;
   he snapped their chains.
15 Let them praise the Lord for his great love
   and for the wonderful things he has done for them.
16 For he broke down their prison gates of bronze;
   he cut apart their bars of iron.

17 Some were fools; they rebelled
   and suffered for their sins.

¹⁸ They couldn't stand the thought of food,
and they were knocking on death's door.
¹⁹ "LORD, help!" they cried in their trouble,
and he saved them from their distress.
²⁰ He sent out his word and healed them,
snatching them from the door of death.
²¹ Let them praise the LORD for his great love
and for the wonderful things he has done for
them.
²² Let them offer sacrifices of thanksgiving
and sing joyfully about his glorious acts.

²³ Some went off to sea in ships,
plying the trade routes of the world.
²⁴ They, too, observed the LORD's power in action,
his impressive works on the deepest seas.
²⁵ He spoke, and the winds rose,
stirring up the waves.
²⁶ Their ships were tossed to the heavens
and plunged again to the depths;
the sailors cringed in terror.
²⁷ They reeled and staggered like drunkards
and were at their wits' end.
²⁸ "LORD, help!" they cried in their trouble,
and he saved them from their distress.

²⁹ He calmed the storm to a whisper
  and stilled the waves.
³⁰ What a blessing was that stillness
  as he brought them safely into harbor!
³¹ Let them praise the LORD for his great love
  and for the wonderful things he has done for them.
³² Let them exalt him publicly before the congregation
  and before the leaders of the nation.

³³ He changes rivers into deserts,
  and springs of water into dry, thirsty land.
³⁴ He turns the fruitful land into salty wastelands,
  because of the wickedness of those who live there.
³⁵ But he also turns deserts into pools of water,
  the dry land into springs of water.
³⁶ He brings the hungry to settle there
  and to build their cities.
³⁷ They sow their fields, plant their vineyards,
  and harvest their bumper crops.
³⁸ How he blesses them!
  They raise large families there,
  and their herds of livestock increase.

³⁹ When they decrease in number and become
    impoverished
  through oppression, trouble, and sorrow,

40 the LORD pours contempt on their princes,
    causing them to wander in trackless wastelands.
41 But he rescues the poor from trouble
    and increases their families like flocks of sheep.
42 The godly will see these things and be glad,
    while the wicked are struck silent.
43 Those who are wise will take all this to heart;
    they will see in our history the faithful love
      of the LORD.

✳ PROVERBS 23

1 While dining with a ruler,
    pay attention to what is put before you.
2 If you are a big eater,
    put a knife to your throat;
3 don't desire all the delicacies,
    for he might be trying to trick you.

4 Don't wear yourself out trying to get rich.
    Be wise enough to know when to quit.
5 In the blink of an eye wealth disappears,
    for it will sprout wings
    and fly away like an eagle.

6 Don't eat with people who are stingy;
    don't desire their delicacies.

7 They are always thinking about how much it costs.
"Eat and drink," they say, but they don't
mean it.
8 You will throw up what little you've eaten,
and your compliments will be wasted.

9 Don't waste your breath on fools,
for they will despise the wisest advice.

10 Don't cheat your neighbor by moving the ancient
boundary markers;
don't take the land of defenseless orphans.
11 For their Redeemer is strong;
he himself will bring their charges against you.

12 Commit yourself to instruction;
listen carefully to words of knowledge.

13 Don't fail to discipline your children.
The rod of punishment won't kill them.
14 Physical discipline
may well save them from death.

15 My child, if your heart is wise,
my own heart will rejoice!
16 Everything in me will celebrate
when you speak what is right.

¹⁷ Don't envy sinners,
    but always continue to fear the LORD.
¹⁸ You will be rewarded for this;
    your hope will not be disappointed.

¹⁹ My child, listen and be wise:
    Keep your heart on the right course.
²⁰ Do not carouse with drunkards
    or feast with gluttons,
²¹ for they are on their way to poverty,
    and too much sleep clothes them in rags.

²² Listen to your father, who gave you life,
    and don't despise your mother when she is old.
²³ Get the truth and never sell it;
    also get wisdom, discipline, and good judgment.
²⁴ The father of godly children has cause for joy.
    What a pleasure to have children who are wise.
²⁵ So give your father and mother joy!
    May she who gave you birth be happy.

²⁶ O my son, give me your heart.
    May your eyes take delight in following my ways.
²⁷ A prostitute is a dangerous trap;
    a promiscuous woman is as dangerous as falling
        into a narrow well.

²⁸ She hides and waits like a robber,
    eager to make more men unfaithful.

²⁹ Who has anguish? Who has sorrow?
    Who is always fighting? Who is always
        complaining?
    Who has unnecessary bruises? Who has
        bloodshot eyes?
³⁰ It is the one who spends long hours in the taverns,
    trying out new drinks.
³¹ Don't gaze at the wine, seeing how red it is,
    how it sparkles in the cup, how smoothly it
        goes down.
³² For in the end it bites like a poisonous snake;
    it stings like a viper.
³³ You will see hallucinations,
    and you will say crazy things.
³⁴ You will stagger like a sailor tossed at sea,
    clinging to a swaying mast.
³⁵ And you will say, "They hit me, but I didn't feel it.
    I didn't even know it when they beat me up.
    When will I wake up
        so I can look for another drink?"

🔥 PSALM 108

A song. A psalm of David.

¹ My heart is confident in you, O God;
    no wonder I can sing your praises with all my heart!
² Wake up, lyre and harp!
    I will wake the dawn with my song.
³ I will thank you, LORD, among all the people.
    I will sing your praises among the nations.
⁴ For your unfailing love is higher than the heavens.
    Your faithfulness reaches to the clouds.
⁵ Be exalted, O God, above the highest heavens.
    May your glory shine over all the earth.

⁶ Now rescue your beloved people.
    Answer and save us by your power.
⁷ God has promised this by his holiness:
  "I will divide up Shechem with joy.
    I will measure out the valley of Succoth.
⁸ Gilead is mine,
    and Manasseh, too.
  Ephraim, my helmet, will produce my warriors,
    and Judah, my scepter, will produce my kings.

⁹ But Moab, my washbasin, will become my servant,
    and I will wipe my feet on Edom
    and shout in triumph over Philistia."

¹⁰ Who will bring me into the fortified city?
    Who will bring me victory over Edom?
¹¹ Have you rejected us, O God?
    Will you no longer march with our armies?
¹² Oh, please help us against our enemies,
    for all human help is useless.
¹³ With God's help we will do mighty things,
    for he will trample down our foes.

🔥 PSALM 109

For the choir director: A psalm of David.

¹ O God, whom I praise,
    don't stand silent and aloof
² while the wicked slander me
    and tell lies about me.
³ They surround me with hateful words
    and fight against me for no reason.
⁴ I love them, but they try to destroy me with
        accusations
    even as I am praying for them!

5 They repay evil for good,
   and hatred for my love.

6 They say, "Get an evil person to turn
      against him.
   Send an accuser to bring him to trial.
7 When his case comes up for judgment,
   let him be pronounced guilty.
   Count his prayers as sins.
8 Let his years be few;
   let someone else take his position.
9 May his children become fatherless,
   and his wife a widow.
10 May his children wander as beggars
   and be driven from their ruined homes.
11 May creditors seize his entire estate,
   and strangers take all he has earned.
12 Let no one be kind to him;
   let no one pity his fatherless children.
13 May all his offspring die.
   May his family name be blotted out in the next
      generation.
14 May the LORD never forget the sins of his fathers;
   may his mother's sins never be erased from the
      record.

¹⁵ May the LORD always remember these sins,
    and may his name disappear from human memory.
¹⁶ For he refused all kindness to others;
    he persecuted the poor and needy,
    and he hounded the brokenhearted to death.
¹⁷ He loved to curse others;
    now you curse him.
  He never blessed others;
    now don't you bless him.
¹⁸ Cursing is as natural to him as his clothing,
    or the water he drinks,
    or the rich food he eats.
¹⁹ Now may his curses return and cling to him like
        clothing;
    may they be tied around him like a belt."

²⁰ May those curses become the LORD's
        punishment
    for my accusers who speak evil of me.
²¹ But deal well with me, O Sovereign LORD,
    for the sake of your own reputation!
  Rescue me
    because you are so faithful and good.
²² For I am poor and needy,
    and my heart is full of pain.

²³ I am fading like a shadow at dusk;
    I am brushed off like a locust.
²⁴ My knees are weak from fasting,
    and I am skin and bones.
²⁵ I am a joke to people everywhere;
    when they see me, they shake their heads
        in scorn.

²⁶ Help me, O LORD my God!
    Save me because of your unfailing love.
²⁷ Let them see that this is your doing,
    that you yourself have done it, LORD.
²⁸ Then let them curse me if they like,
    but you will bless me!
When they attack me, they will be disgraced!
    But I, your servant, will go right on
        rejoicing!
²⁹ May my accusers be clothed with disgrace;
    may their humiliation cover them like
        a cloak.
³⁰ But I will give repeated thanks to the LORD,
    praising him to everyone.
³¹ For he stands beside the needy,
    ready to save them from those who condemn
        them.

❧ PSALM 110

A psalm of David.

1 The LORD said to my Lord,
  "Sit in the place of honor at my right hand
 until I humble your enemies,
  making them a footstool under your feet."

2 The LORD will extend your powerful kingdom from
   Jerusalem;
  you will rule over your enemies.
3 When you go to war,
  your people will serve you willingly.
 You are arrayed in holy garments,
  and your strength will be renewed each day like
   the morning dew.

4 The LORD has taken an oath and will not break
   his vow:
  "You are a priest forever in the order of
   Melchizedek."

5 The Lord stands at your right hand to protect you.
  He will strike down many kings when his anger
   erupts.
6 He will punish the nations
  and fill their lands with corpses;

he will shatter heads over the whole earth.

7 But he himself will be refreshed from brooks along
the way.

He will be victorious.

🔥 PSALM 111

1 Praise the LORD!

I will thank the LORD with all my heart
as I meet with his godly people.

2 How amazing are the deeds of the LORD!
All who delight in him should ponder them.

3 Everything he does reveals his glory and majesty.
His righteousness never fails.

4 He causes us to remember his wonderful works.
How gracious and merciful is our LORD!

5 He gives food to those who fear him;
he always remembers his covenant.

6 He has shown his great power to his people
by giving them the lands of other nations.

7 All he does is just and good,
and all his commandments are trustworthy.

8 They are forever true,
to be obeyed faithfully and with integrity.

⁹ He has paid a full ransom for his people.
   He has guaranteed his covenant with them
      forever.
   What a holy, awe-inspiring name he has!
¹⁰ Fear of the LORD is the foundation of true wisdom.
   All who obey his commandments will grow
      in wisdom.

Praise him forever!

✳ PROVERBS 24

¹ Don't envy evil people
   or desire their company.
² For their hearts plot violence,
   and their words always stir up trouble.

³ A house is built by wisdom
   and becomes strong through good sense.
⁴ Through knowledge its rooms are filled
   with all sorts of precious riches and valuables.

⁵ The wise are mightier than the strong,
   and those with knowledge grow stronger and
      stronger.
⁶ So don't go to war without wise guidance;
   victory depends on having many advisers.

7 Wisdom is too lofty for fools.
    Among leaders at the city gate, they have
        nothing to say.

8 A person who plans evil
    will get a reputation as a troublemaker.
9 The schemes of a fool are sinful;
    everyone detests a mocker.

10 If you fail under pressure,
    your strength is too small.

11 Rescue those who are unjustly sentenced to die;
    save them as they stagger to their death.
12 Don't excuse yourself by saying, "Look, we didn't
        know."
    For God understands all hearts, and he sees you.
He who guards your soul knows you knew.
    He will repay all people as their actions deserve.

13 My child, eat honey, for it is good,
    and the honeycomb is sweet to the taste.
14 In the same way, wisdom is sweet to your soul.
    If you find it, you will have a bright future,
    and your hopes will not be cut short.

15 Don't wait in ambush at the home of the godly,
    and don't raid the house where the godly live.

¹⁶ The godly may trip seven times, but they will get
    up again.
    But one disaster is enough to overthrow the wicked.

¹⁷ Don't rejoice when your enemies fall;
    don't be happy when they stumble.
¹⁸ For the LORD will be displeased with you
    and will turn his anger away from them.

¹⁹ Don't fret because of evildoers;
    don't envy the wicked.
²⁰ For evil people have no future;
    the light of the wicked will be snuffed out.

²¹ My child, fear the LORD and the king.
    Don't associate with rebels,
²²   for disaster will hit them suddenly.
    Who knows what punishment will come
        from the LORD and the king?

²³ Here are some further sayings of the wise:

    It is wrong to show favoritism when passing
        judgment.
²⁴ A judge who says to the wicked, "You are innocent,"
    will be cursed by many people and denounced by
        the nations.

25 But it will go well for those who convict
        the guilty;
    rich blessings will be showered on them.

26 An honest answer
    is like a kiss of friendship.

27 Do your planning and prepare your fields
    before building your house.

28 Don't testify against your neighbors without cause;
    don't lie about them.
29 And don't say, "Now I can pay them back for what
        they've done to me!
    I'll get even with them!"

30 I walked by the field of a lazy person,
    the vineyard of one with no common sense.
31 I saw that it was overgrown with nettles.
    It was covered with weeds,
    and its walls were broken down.
32 Then, as I looked and thought about it,
    I learned this lesson:
33 A little extra sleep, a little more slumber,
    a little folding of the hands to rest—
34 then poverty will pounce on you like a bandit;
    scarcity will attack you like an armed robber.

🔥 PSALM 112

¹ Praise the LORD!

How joyful are those who fear the LORD
   and delight in obeying his commands.
² Their children will be successful everywhere;
   an entire generation of godly people will be
      blessed.
³ They themselves will be wealthy,
   and their good deeds will last forever.
⁴ Light shines in the darkness for the godly.
   They are generous, compassionate, and
      righteous.
⁵ Good comes to those who lend money generously
   and conduct their business fairly.
⁶ Such people will not be overcome by evil.
   Those who are righteous will be long
      remembered.
⁷ They do not fear bad news;
   they confidently trust the LORD to care for them.
⁸ They are confident and fearless
   and can face their foes triumphantly.

⁹ They share freely and give generously to those
        in need.
    Their good deeds will be remembered forever.
    They will have influence and honor.
¹⁰ The wicked will see this and be infuriated.
    They will grind their teeth in anger;
        they will slink away, their hopes thwarted.

🔥 PSALM 113

¹ Praise the LORD!

  Yes, give praise, O servants of the LORD.
    Praise the name of the LORD!
² Blessed be the name of the LORD
    now and forever.
³ Everywhere—from east to west—
    praise the name of the LORD.
⁴ For the LORD is high above the nations;
    his glory is higher than the heavens.

⁵ Who can be compared with the LORD our God,
    who is enthroned on high?
⁶ He stoops to look down
    on heaven and on earth.
⁷ He lifts the poor from the dust
    and the needy from the garbage dump.

8 He sets them among princes,
   even the princes of his own people!
9 He gives the childless woman a family,
   making her a happy mother.

Praise the LORD!

🔥 PSALM 114

1 When the Israelites escaped from Egypt—
   when the family of Jacob left that foreign land—
2 the land of Judah became God's sanctuary,
   and Israel became his kingdom.

3 The Red Sea saw them coming and hurried out
      of their way!
   The water of the Jordan River turned away.
4 The mountains skipped like rams,
   the hills like lambs!
5 What's wrong, Red Sea, that made you hurry out
      of their way?
   What happened, Jordan River, that you turned
      away?
6 Why, mountains, did you skip like rams?
   Why, hills, like lambs?
7 Tremble, O earth, at the presence of the Lord,
   at the presence of the God of Jacob.

⁸ He turned the rock into a pool of water;
  yes, a spring of water flowed from solid rock.

❦ PSALM 115

¹ Not to us, O LORD, not to us,
  but to your name goes all the glory
  for your unfailing love and faithfulness.
² Why let the nations say,
  "Where is their God?"
³ Our God is in the heavens,
  and he does as he wishes.
⁴ Their idols are merely things of silver and gold,
  shaped by human hands.
⁵ They have mouths but cannot speak,
  and eyes but cannot see.
⁶ They have ears but cannot hear,
  and noses but cannot smell.
⁷ They have hands but cannot feel,
  and feet but cannot walk,
  and throats but cannot make a sound.
⁸ And those who make idols are just like them,
  as are all who trust in them.

⁹ O Israel, trust the LORD!
  He is your helper and your shield.

¹⁰ O priests, descendants of Aaron, trust the LORD!
   He is your helper and your shield.
¹¹ All you who fear the LORD, trust the LORD!
   He is your helper and your shield.

¹² The LORD remembers us and will bless us.
   He will bless the people of Israel
   and bless the priests, the descendants of Aaron.
¹³ He will bless those who fear the LORD,
   both great and lowly.

¹⁴ May the LORD richly bless
   both you and your children.
¹⁵ May you be blessed by the LORD,
   who made heaven and earth.
¹⁶ The heavens belong to the LORD,
   but he has given the earth to all humanity.
¹⁷ The dead cannot sing praises to the LORD,
   for they have gone into the silence of the grave.
¹⁸ But we can praise the LORD
   both now and forever!

   Praise the LORD!

🕯 PSALM 116

¹ I love the LORD because he hears my voice
   and my prayer for mercy.

² Because he bends down to listen,
   I will pray as long as I have breath!
³ Death wrapped its ropes around me;
   the terrors of the grave overtook me.
   I saw only trouble and sorrow.
⁴ Then I called on the name of the LORD:
   "Please, LORD, save me!"
⁵ How kind the LORD is! How good he is!
   So merciful, this God of ours!
⁶ The LORD protects those of childlike faith;
   I was facing death, and he saved me.
⁷ Let my soul be at rest again,
   for the LORD has been good to me.
⁸ He has saved me from death,
   my eyes from tears,
   my feet from stumbling.
⁹ And so I walk in the LORD's presence
   as I live here on earth!
¹⁰ I believed in you, so I said,
   "I am deeply troubled, LORD."
¹¹ In my anxiety I cried out to you,
   "These people are all liars!"
¹² What can I offer the LORD
   for all he has done for me?

13 I will lift up the cup of salvation
   and praise the LORD's name for saving me.
14 I will keep my promises to the LORD
   in the presence of all his people.

15 The LORD cares deeply
   when his loved ones die.
16 O LORD, I am your servant;
   yes, I am your servant, born into your household;
   you have freed me from my chains.
17 I will offer you a sacrifice of thanksgiving
   and call on the name of the LORD.
18 I will fulfill my vows to the LORD
   in the presence of all his people—
19 in the house of the LORD
   in the heart of Jerusalem.

   Praise the LORD!

❦ PSALM 117

1 Praise the LORD, all you nations.
   Praise him, all you people of the earth.
2 For his unfailing love for us is powerful;
   the LORD's faithfulness endures forever.

   Praise the LORD!

🔥 Psalm 118

1 Give thanks to the LORD, for he is good!
　His faithful love endures forever.

2 Let all Israel repeat:
　"His faithful love endures forever."
3 Let Aaron's descendants, the priests, repeat:
　"His faithful love endures forever."
4 Let all who fear the LORD repeat:
　"His faithful love endures forever."

5 In my distress I prayed to the LORD,
　and the LORD answered me and set me free.
6 The LORD is for me, so I will have no fear.
　What can mere people do to me?
7 Yes, the LORD is for me; he will help me.
　I will look in triumph at those who hate me.
8 It is better to take refuge in the LORD
　than to trust in people.
9 It is better to take refuge in the LORD
　than to trust in princes.

10 Though hostile nations surrounded me,
　I destroyed them all with the authority of
　　the LORD.
11 Yes, they surrounded and attacked me,

but I destroyed them all with the authority
   of the Lord.
12 They swarmed around me like bees;
   they blazed against me like a crackling fire.
   But I destroyed them all with the authority
   of the Lord.
13 My enemies did their best to kill me,
   but the Lord rescued me.
14 The Lord is my strength and my song;
   he has given me victory.
15 Songs of joy and victory are sung in the camp
   of the godly.
   The strong right arm of the Lord has done
   glorious things!
16 The strong right arm of the Lord is raised in
   triumph.
   The strong right arm of the Lord has done
   glorious things!
17 I will not die; instead, I will live
   to tell what the Lord has done.
18 The Lord has punished me severely,
   but he did not let me die.

19 Open for me the gates where the righteous enter,
   and I will go in and thank the Lord.

²⁰ These gates lead to the presence of
    the LORD,
    and the godly enter there.
²¹ I thank you for answering my prayer
    and giving me victory!

²² The stone that the builders rejected
    has now become the cornerstone.
²³ This is the LORD's doing,
    and it is wonderful to see.
²⁴ This is the day the LORD has made.
    We will rejoice and be glad in it.
²⁵ Please, LORD, please save us.
    Please, LORD, please give us success.
²⁶ Bless the one who comes in the name
    of the LORD.
    We bless you from the house of the LORD.
²⁷ The LORD is God, shining upon us.
    Take the sacrifice and bind it with cords
    on the altar.
²⁸ You are my God, and I will praise you!
    You are my God, and I will exalt you!

²⁹ Give thanks to the LORD, for he is good!
    His faithful love endures forever.

✳ PROVERBS 25

These are more proverbs of Solomon, collected by the advisers of King Hezekiah of Judah.

² It is God's privilege to conceal things
  and the king's privilege to discover them.

³ No one can comprehend the height of heaven, the
    depth of the earth,
  or all that goes on in the king's mind!

⁴ Remove the impurities from silver,
  and the sterling will be ready for the silversmith.
⁵ Remove the wicked from the king's court,
  and his reign will be made secure by justice.

⁶ Don't demand an audience with the king
  or push for a place among the great.
⁷ It's better to wait for an invitation to the head table
  than to be sent away in public disgrace.

  Just because you've seen something,
⁸   don't be in a hurry to go to court.
  For what will you do in the end
    if your neighbor deals you a shameful defeat?

⁹ When arguing with your neighbor,
  don't betray another person's secret.

¹⁰ Others may accuse you of gossip,
    and you will never regain your good reputation.

¹¹ Timely advice is lovely,
    like golden apples in a silver basket.

¹² To one who listens, valid criticism
    is like a gold earring or other gold jewelry.

¹³ Trustworthy messengers refresh like snow in
        summer.
    They revive the spirit of their employer.

¹⁴ A person who promises a gift but doesn't give it
    is like clouds and wind that bring no rain.

¹⁵ Patience can persuade a prince,
    and soft speech can break bones.

¹⁶ Do you like honey?
    Don't eat too much, or it will make you sick!

¹⁷ Don't visit your neighbors too often,
    or you will wear out your welcome.

¹⁸ Telling lies about others
    is as harmful as hitting them with an ax,
  wounding them with a sword,
    or shooting them with a sharp arrow.

¹⁹ Putting confidence in an unreliable person in times
     of trouble
          is like chewing with a broken tooth or walking
          on a lame foot.

²⁰ Singing cheerful songs to a person with a heavy
     heart
          is like taking someone's coat in cold weather
          or pouring vinegar in a wound.

²¹ If your enemies are hungry, give them food to eat.
          If they are thirsty, give them water to drink.
²² You will heap burning coals of shame on their
     heads,
          and the LORD will reward you.

²³ As surely as a north wind brings rain,
          so a gossiping tongue causes anger!

²⁴ It's better to live alone in the corner of an attic
          than with a quarrelsome wife in a lovely home.

²⁵ Good news from far away
          is like cold water to the thirsty.

²⁶ If the godly give in to the wicked,
          it's like polluting a fountain or muddying
          a spring.

²⁷ It's not good to eat too much honey,
    and it's not good to seek honors for yourself.

²⁸ A person without self-control
    is like a city with broken-down walls.

❧ PSALM 119

Aleph

1 Joyful are people of integrity,
    who follow the instructions of the LORD.
2 Joyful are those who obey his laws
    and search for him with all their hearts.
3 They do not compromise with evil,
    and they walk only in his paths.
4 You have charged us
    to keep your commandments carefully.
5 Oh, that my actions would consistently
    reflect your decrees!
6 Then I will not be ashamed
    when I compare my life with your commands.
7 As I learn your righteous regulations,
    I will thank you by living as I should!
8 I will obey your decrees.
    Please don't give up on me!

Beth

9 How can a young person stay pure?
    By obeying your word.

¹⁰ I have tried hard to find you—
    don't let me wander from your commands.
¹¹ I have hidden your word in my heart,
    that I might not sin against you.
¹² I praise you, O LORD;
    teach me your decrees.
¹³ I have recited aloud
    all the regulations you have given us.
¹⁴ I have rejoiced in your laws
    as much as in riches.
¹⁵ I will study your commandments
    and reflect on your ways.
¹⁶ I will delight in your decrees
    and not forget your word.

Gimel

¹⁷ Be good to your servant,
    that I may live and obey your word.
¹⁸ Open my eyes to see
    the wonderful truths in your instructions.
¹⁹ I am only a foreigner in the land.
    Don't hide your commands from me!
²⁰ I am always overwhelmed
    with a desire for your regulations.
²¹ You rebuke the arrogant;

those who wander from your commands are
    cursed.
²² Don't let them scorn and insult me,
    for I have obeyed your laws.
²³ Even princes sit and speak against me,
    but I will meditate on your decrees.
²⁴ Your laws please me;
    they give me wise advice.

Daleth

²⁵ I lie in the dust;
    revive me by your word.
²⁶ I told you my plans, and you answered.
    Now teach me your decrees.
²⁷ Help me understand the meaning of your
      commandments,
    and I will meditate on your wonderful deeds.
²⁸ I weep with sorrow;
    encourage me by your word.
²⁹ Keep me from lying to myself;
    give me the privilege of knowing your
      instructions.
³⁰ I have chosen to be faithful;
    I have determined to live by your regulations.

³¹ I cling to your laws.
    Lord, don't let me be put to shame!
³² I will pursue your commands,
    for you expand my understanding.

He

³³ Teach me your decrees, O Lord;
    I will keep them to the end.
³⁴ Give me understanding and I will obey your
        instructions;
    I will put them into practice with all my heart.
³⁵ Make me walk along the path of your
        commands,
    for that is where my happiness is found.
³⁶ Give me an eagerness for your laws
    rather than a love for money!
³⁷ Turn my eyes from worthless things,
    and give me life through your word.
³⁸ Reassure me of your promise,
    made to those who fear you.
³⁹ Help me abandon my shameful ways;
    for your regulations are good.
⁴⁰ I long to obey your commandments!
    Renew my life with your goodness.

Waw

41 LORD, give me your unfailing love,
     the salvation that you promised me.
42 Then I can answer those who taunt me,
     for I trust in your word.
43 Do not snatch your word of truth from me,
     for your regulations are my only hope.
44 I will keep on obeying your instructions
     forever and ever.
45 I will walk in freedom,
     for I have devoted myself to your
          commandments.
46 I will speak to kings about your laws,
     and I will not be ashamed.
47 How I delight in your commands!
     How I love them!
48 I honor and love your commands.
     I meditate on your decrees.

Zayin

49 Remember your promise to me;
     it is my only hope.
50 Your promise revives me;
     it comforts me in all my troubles.

⁵¹ The proud hold me in utter contempt,
  but I do not turn away from your instructions.
⁵² I meditate on your age-old regulations;
  O Lᴏʀᴅ, they comfort me.
⁵³ I become furious with the wicked,
  because they reject your instructions.
⁵⁴ Your decrees have been the theme of my songs
  wherever I have lived.
⁵⁵ I reflect at night on who you are, O Lᴏʀᴅ;
  therefore, I obey your instructions.
⁵⁶ This is how I spend my life:
  obeying your commandments.

Heth

⁵⁷ Lᴏʀᴅ, you are mine!
  I promise to obey your words!
⁵⁸ With all my heart I want your blessings.
  Be merciful as you promised.
⁵⁹ I pondered the direction of my life,
  and I turned to follow your laws.
⁶⁰ I will hurry, without delay,
  to obey your commands.
⁶¹ Evil people try to drag me into sin,
  but I am firmly anchored to your instructions.

⁶² I rise at midnight to thank you
    for your just regulations.
⁶³ I am a friend to anyone who fears you—
    anyone who obeys your commandments.
⁶⁴ O LORD, your unfailing love fills the earth;
    teach me your decrees.

Teth

⁶⁵ You have done many good things for me, LORD,
    just as you promised.
⁶⁶ I believe in your commands;
    now teach me good judgment and knowledge.
⁶⁷ I used to wander off until you disciplined me;
    but now I closely follow your word.
⁶⁸ You are good and do only good;
    teach me your decrees.
⁶⁹ Arrogant people smear me with lies,
    but in truth I obey your commandments with all
        my heart.
⁷⁰ Their hearts are dull and stupid,
    but I delight in your instructions.
⁷¹ My suffering was good for me,
    for it taught me to pay attention to your decrees.
⁷² Your instructions are more valuable to me
    than millions in gold and silver.

Yodh

73 You made me; you created me.
Now give me the sense to follow your
commands.

74 May all who fear you find in me a cause for joy,
for I have put my hope in your word.

75 I know, O LORD, that your regulations are fair;
you disciplined me because I needed it.

76 Now let your unfailing love comfort me,
just as you promised me, your servant.

77 Surround me with your tender mercies so I may live,
for your instructions are my delight.

78 Bring disgrace upon the arrogant people who lied
about me;
meanwhile, I will concentrate on your
commandments.

79 Let me be united with all who fear you,
with those who know your laws.

80 May I be blameless in keeping your decrees;
then I will never be ashamed.

Kaph

81 I am worn out waiting for your rescue,
but I have put my hope in your word.

⁸² My eyes are straining to see your promises come true.
    When will you comfort me?
⁸³ I am shriveled like a wineskin in the smoke,
    but I have not forgotten to obey your decrees.
⁸⁴ How long must I wait?
    When will you punish those who persecute me?
⁸⁵ These arrogant people who hate your instructions
    have dug deep pits to trap me.
⁸⁶ All your commands are trustworthy.
    Protect me from those who hunt me down
        without cause.
⁸⁷ They almost finished me off,
    but I refused to abandon your commandments.
⁸⁸ In your unfailing love, spare my life;
    then I can continue to obey your laws.

Lamedh

⁸⁹ Your eternal word, O Lord,
    stands firm in heaven.
⁹⁰ Your faithfulness extends to every generation,
    as enduring as the earth you created.
⁹¹ Your regulations remain true to this day,
    for everything serves your plans.
⁹² If your instructions hadn't sustained me with joy,
    I would have died in my misery.

[93] I will never forget your commandments,
    for by them you give me life.
[94] I am yours; rescue me!
    For I have worked hard at obeying your
        commandments.
[95] Though the wicked hide along the way to kill me,
    I will quietly keep my mind on your laws.
[96] Even perfection has its limits,
    but your commands have no limit.

Mem

[97] Oh, how I love your instructions!
    I think about them all day long.
[98] Your commands make me wiser than my enemies,
    for they are my constant guide.
[99] Yes, I have more insight than my teachers,
    for I am always thinking of your laws.
[100] I am even wiser than my elders,
    for I have kept your commandments.
[101] I have refused to walk on any evil path,
    so that I may remain obedient to your word.
[102] I haven't turned away from your regulations,
    for you have taught me well.
[103] How sweet your words taste to me;
    they are sweeter than honey.

[104] Your commandments give me understanding;
    no wonder I hate every false way of life.

Nun

[105] Your word is a lamp to guide my feet
    and a light for my path.
[106] I've promised it once, and I'll promise it again:
    I will obey your righteous regulations.
[107] I have suffered much, O LORD;
    restore my life again as you promised.
[108] LORD, accept my offering of praise,
    and teach me your regulations.
[109] My life constantly hangs in the balance,
    but I will not stop obeying your instructions.
[110] The wicked have set their traps for me,
    but I will not turn from your
        commandments.
[111] Your laws are my treasure;
    they are my heart's delight.
[112] I am determined to keep your decrees
    to the very end.

Samekh

[113] I hate those with divided loyalties,
    but I love your instructions.

¹¹⁴ You are my refuge and my shield;
>   your word is my source of hope.
¹¹⁵ Get out of my life, you evil-minded people,
>   for I intend to obey the commands of my God.
¹¹⁶ LORD, sustain me as you promised, that I may live!
>   Do not let my hope be crushed.
¹¹⁷ Sustain me, and I will be rescued;
>   then I will meditate continually on your decrees.
¹¹⁸ But you have rejected all who stray from your
>   decrees.
>   They are only fooling themselves.
¹¹⁹ You skim off the wicked of the earth like scum;
>   no wonder I love to obey your laws!
¹²⁰ I tremble in fear of you;
>   I stand in awe of your regulations.

Ayin

¹²¹ Don't leave me to the mercy of my enemies,
>   for I have done what is just and right.
¹²² Please guarantee a blessing for me.
>   Don't let the arrogant oppress me!
¹²³ My eyes strain to see your rescue,
>   to see the truth of your promise fulfilled.

[124] I am your servant; deal with me in unfailing love,
   and teach me your decrees.
[125] Give discernment to me, your servant;
   then I will understand your laws.
[126] LORD, it is time for you to act,
   for these evil people have violated your
      instructions.
[127] Truly, I love your commands
   more than gold, even the finest gold.
[128] Each of your commandments is right.
   That is why I hate every false way.

Pe

[129] Your laws are wonderful.
   No wonder I obey them!
[130] The teaching of your word gives light,
   so even the simple can understand.
[131] I pant with expectation,
   longing for your commands.
[132] Come and show me your mercy,
   as you do for all who love your name.
[133] Guide my steps by your word,
   so I will not be overcome by evil.
[134] Ransom me from the oppression of evil people;
   then I can obey your commandments.

135 Look upon me with love;
>   teach me your decrees.
136 Rivers of tears gush from my eyes
>   because people disobey your instructions.

Tsadhe

137 O LORD, you are righteous,
>   and your regulations are fair.
138 Your laws are perfect
>   and completely trustworthy.
139 I am overwhelmed with indignation,
>   for my enemies have disregarded your words.
140 Your promises have been thoroughly tested;
>   that is why I love them so much.
141 I am insignificant and despised,
>   but I don't forget your commandments.
142 Your justice is eternal,
>   and your instructions are perfectly true.
143 As pressure and stress bear down on me,
>   I find joy in your commands.
144 Your laws are always right;
>   help me to understand them so I may live.

Qoph

145 I pray with all my heart; answer me, LORD!
>   I will obey your decrees.

¹⁴⁶ I cry out to you; rescue me,
    that I may obey your laws.
¹⁴⁷ I rise early, before the sun is up;
    I cry out for help and put my hope in your words.
¹⁴⁸ I stay awake through the night,
    thinking about your promise.
¹⁴⁹ In your faithful love, O LORD, hear my cry;
    let me be revived by following your regulations.
¹⁵⁰ Lawless people are coming to attack me;
    they live far from your instructions.
¹⁵¹ But you are near, O LORD,
    and all your commands are true.
¹⁵² I have known from my earliest days
    that your laws will last forever.

Resh

¹⁵³ Look upon my suffering and rescue me,
    for I have not forgotten your instructions.
¹⁵⁴ Argue my case; take my side!
    Protect my life as you promised.
¹⁵⁵ The wicked are far from rescue,
    for they do not bother with your decrees.
¹⁵⁶ LORD, how great is your mercy;
    let me be revived by following your regulations.

¹⁵⁷ Many persecute and trouble me,
    yet I have not swerved from your laws.
¹⁵⁸ Seeing these traitors makes me sick at heart,
    because they care nothing for your word.
¹⁵⁹ See how I love your commandments, LORD.
    Give back my life because of your unfailing love.
¹⁶⁰ The very essence of your words is truth;
    all your just regulations will stand forever.

Shin

¹⁶¹ Powerful people harass me without cause,
    but my heart trembles only at your word.
¹⁶² I rejoice in your word
    like one who discovers a great treasure.
¹⁶³ I hate and abhor all falsehood,
    but I love your instructions.
¹⁶⁴ I will praise you seven times a day
    because all your regulations are just.
¹⁶⁵ Those who love your instructions have great peace
    and do not stumble.
¹⁶⁶ I long for your rescue, LORD,
    so I have obeyed your commands.
¹⁶⁷ I have obeyed your laws,
    for I love them very much.

168 Yes, I obey your commandments and laws
    because you know everything I do.

Taw

169 O LORD, listen to my cry;
    give me the discerning mind you
        promised.
170 Listen to my prayer;
    rescue me as you promised.
171 Let praise flow from my lips,
    for you have taught me your decrees.
172 Let my tongue sing about your word,
    for all your commands are right.
173 Give me a helping hand,
    for I have chosen to follow your
        commandments.
174 O LORD, I have longed for your rescue,
    and your instructions are my delight.
175 Let me live so I can praise you,
    and may your regulations help me.
176 I have wandered away like a lost sheep;
    come and find me,
    for I have not forgotten your commands.

✳ PROVERBS 26

¹ Honor is no more associated with fools
    than snow with summer or rain with harvest.

² Like a fluttering sparrow or a darting swallow,
    an undeserved curse will not land on its intended
        victim.

³ Guide a horse with a whip, a donkey with a bridle,
    and a fool with a rod to his back!

⁴ Don't answer the foolish arguments of fools,
    or you will become as foolish as they are.

⁵ Be sure to answer the foolish arguments of fools,
    or they will become wise in their own
        estimation.

⁶ Trusting a fool to convey a message
    is like cutting off one's feet or drinking poison!

⁷ A proverb in the mouth of a fool
    is as useless as a paralyzed leg.

⁸ Honoring a fool
    is as foolish as tying a stone to a slingshot.

⁹ A proverb in the mouth of a fool
    is like a thorny branch brandished by a drunk.

¹⁰ An employer who hires a fool or a bystander
   is like an archer who shoots at random.

¹¹ As a dog returns to its vomit,
   so a fool repeats his foolishness.

¹² There is more hope for fools
   than for people who think they are wise.

¹³ The lazy person claims, "There's a lion on
   the road!
   Yes, I'm sure there's a lion out there!"

¹⁴ As a door swings back and forth on its hinges,
   so the lazy person turns over in bed.

¹⁵ Lazy people take food in their hand
   but don't even lift it to their mouth.

¹⁶ Lazy people consider themselves smarter
   than seven wise counselors.

¹⁷ Interfering in someone else's argument
   is as foolish as yanking a dog's ears.

¹⁸ Just as damaging
   as a madman shooting a deadly weapon
¹⁹ is someone who lies to a friend
   and then says, "I was only joking."

20 Fire goes out without wood,
   and quarrels disappear when gossip stops.

21 A quarrelsome person starts fights
   as easily as hot embers light charcoal or fire
      lights wood.

22 Rumors are dainty morsels
   that sink deep into one's heart.

23 Smooth words may hide a wicked heart,
   just as a pretty glaze covers a clay pot.

24 People may cover their hatred with pleasant words,
   but they're deceiving you.

25 They pretend to be kind, but don't believe them.
   Their hearts are full of many evils.

26 While their hatred may be concealed by trickery,
   their wrongdoing will be exposed in public.

27 If you set a trap for others,
   you will get caught in it yourself.
   If you roll a boulder down on others,
   it will crush you instead.

28 A lying tongue hates its victims,
   and flattering words cause ruin.

DAY TWENTY-SEVEN

🔥 PSALM 120

A song for pilgrims ascending to Jerusalem.

¹ I took my troubles to the LORD;
    I cried out to him, and he answered my prayer.
² Rescue me, O LORD, from liars
    and from all deceitful people.
³ O deceptive tongue, what will God do to you?
    How will he increase your punishment?
⁴ You will be pierced with sharp arrows
    and burned with glowing coals.

⁵ How I suffer in far-off Meshech.
    It pains me to live in distant Kedar.
⁶ I am tired of living
    among people who hate peace.
⁷ I search for peace;
    but when I speak of peace, they want war!

🔥 PSALM 121

A song for pilgrims ascending to Jerusalem.

¹ I look up to the mountains—
    does my help come from there?

² My help comes from the LORD,
    who made heaven and earth!

³ He will not let you stumble;
    the one who watches over you will not slumber.
⁴ Indeed, he who watches over Israel
    never slumbers or sleeps.

⁵ The LORD himself watches over you!
    The LORD stands beside you as your protective
        shade.
⁶ The sun will not harm you by day,
    nor the moon at night.

⁷ The LORD keeps you from all harm
    and watches over your life.
⁸ The LORD keeps watch over you as you come
        and go,
    both now and forever.

❧ PSALM 122

A song for pilgrims ascending to Jerusalem. A psalm of David.

¹ I was glad when they said to me,
    "Let us go to the house of the LORD."
² And now here we are,
    standing inside your gates, O Jerusalem.

³ Jerusalem is a well-built city;
  its seamless walls cannot be breached.
⁴ All the tribes of Israel—the LORD's people—
  make their pilgrimage here.
  They come to give thanks to the name of the LORD,
  as the law requires of Israel.
⁵ Here stand the thrones where judgment is given,
  the thrones of the dynasty of David.

⁶ Pray for peace in Jerusalem.
  May all who love this city prosper.
⁷ O Jerusalem, may there be peace within your walls
  and prosperity in your palaces.
⁸ For the sake of my family and friends, I will say,
  "May you have peace."
⁹ For the sake of the house of the LORD our God,
  I will seek what is best for you, O Jerusalem.

❧ PSALM 123

A song for pilgrims ascending to Jerusalem.

¹ I lift my eyes to you,
  O God, enthroned in heaven.
² We keep looking to the LORD our God for his
    mercy,
  just as servants keep their eyes on their master,

as a slave girl watches her mistress for the
    slightest signal.
3 Have mercy on us, LORD, have mercy,
    for we have had our fill of contempt.
4 We have had more than our fill of the scoffing
    of the proud
    and the contempt of the arrogant.

🕯 PSALM 124

A song for pilgrims ascending to Jerusalem. A psalm of David.

1 What if the LORD had not been on our side?
    Let all Israel repeat:
2 What if the LORD had not been on our side
    when people attacked us?
3 They would have swallowed us alive
    in their burning anger.
4 The waters would have engulfed us;
    a torrent would have overwhelmed us.
5 Yes, the raging waters of their fury
    would have overwhelmed our very lives.

6 Praise the LORD,
    who did not let their teeth tear us apart!
7 We escaped like a bird from a hunter's trap.
    The trap is broken, and we are free!

⁸ Our help is from the LORD,
   who made heaven and earth.

🔥 PSALM 125

A song for pilgrims ascending to Jerusalem.

¹ Those who trust in the LORD are as secure as
      Mount Zion;
   they will not be defeated but will endure forever.
² Just as the mountains surround Jerusalem,
   so the LORD surrounds his people, both now and
      forever.
³ The wicked will not rule the land of the godly,
   for then the godly might be tempted to do
      wrong.
⁴ O LORD, do good to those who are good,
   whose hearts are in tune with you.
⁵ But banish those who turn to crooked ways, O LORD.
   Take them away with those who do evil.

May Israel have peace!

🔥 PSALM 126

A song for pilgrims ascending to Jerusalem.

¹ When the LORD brought back his exiles to Jerusalem,
   it was like a dream!

² We were filled with laughter,
  and we sang for joy.
And the other nations said,
  "What amazing things the LORD has done
    for them."
³ Yes, the LORD has done amazing things for us!
  What joy!

⁴ Restore our fortunes, LORD,
  as streams renew the desert.
⁵ Those who plant in tears
  will harvest with shouts of joy.
⁶ They weep as they go to plant their seed,
  but they sing as they return with the harvest.

🔥 PSALM 127

A song for pilgrims ascending to Jerusalem. A psalm of Solomon.

¹ Unless the LORD builds a house,
  the work of the builders is wasted.
Unless the LORD protects a city,
  guarding it with sentries will do no good.
² It is useless for you to work so hard
  from early morning until late at night,
anxiously working for food to eat;
  for God gives rest to his loved ones.

³ Children are a gift from the LORD;
 they are a reward from him.
⁴ Children born to a young man
 are like arrows in a warrior's hands.
⁵ How joyful is the man whose quiver is full of them!
 He will not be put to shame when he confronts
 his accusers at the city gates.

🔥 PSALM 128

A song for pilgrims ascending to Jerusalem.

¹ How joyful are those who fear the LORD—
 all who follow his ways!
² You will enjoy the fruit of your labor.
 How joyful and prosperous you will be!
³ Your wife will be like a fruitful grapevine,
 flourishing within your home.
 Your children will be like vigorous young olive trees
 as they sit around your table.
⁴ That is the LORD's blessing
 for those who fear him.

⁵ May the LORD continually bless you from Zion.
 May you see Jerusalem prosper as long as you live.
⁶ May you live to enjoy your grandchildren.
 May Israel have peace!

🌿 PSALM 129

A song for pilgrims ascending to Jerusalem.

¹ From my earliest youth my enemies have
persecuted me.
Let all Israel repeat this:
² From my earliest youth my enemies have
persecuted me,
but they have never defeated me.
³ My back is covered with cuts,
as if a farmer had plowed long furrows.
⁴ But the Lord is good;
he has cut me free from the ropes of the
ungodly.

⁵ May all who hate Jerusalem
be turned back in shameful defeat.
⁶ May they be as useless as grass on a rooftop,
turning yellow when only half grown,
⁷ ignored by the harvester,
despised by the binder.
⁸ And may those who pass by
refuse to give them this blessing:
"The Lord bless you;
we bless you in the Lord's name."

✳ PROVERBS 27

¹ Don't brag about tomorrow,
   since you don't know what the day will bring.

² Let someone else praise you, not your own
      mouth—
   a stranger, not your own lips.

³ A stone is heavy and sand is weighty,
   but the resentment caused by a fool is even
      heavier.

⁴ Anger is cruel, and wrath is like a flood,
   but jealousy is even more dangerous.

⁵ An open rebuke
   is better than hidden love!

⁶ Wounds from a sincere friend
   are better than many kisses from an enemy.

⁷ A person who is full refuses honey,
   but even bitter food tastes sweet to the hungry.

⁸ A person who strays from home
   is like a bird that strays from its nest.

⁹ The heartfelt counsel of a friend
   is as sweet as perfume and incense.

¹⁰ Never abandon a friend—
  either yours or your father's.
 When disaster strikes, you won't have to ask your
   brother for assistance.
  It's better to go to a neighbor than to a brother
   who lives far away.

¹¹ Be wise, my child, and make my heart glad.
  Then I will be able to answer my critics.

¹² A prudent person foresees danger and takes
   precautions.
  The simpleton goes blindly on and suffers
   the consequences.

¹³ Get security from someone who guarantees
   a stranger's debt.
  Get a deposit if he does it for foreigners.

¹⁴ A loud and cheerful greeting early in the morning
   will be taken as a curse!

¹⁵ A quarrelsome wife is as annoying
   as constant dripping on a rainy day.
¹⁶ Stopping her complaints is like trying to stop
   the wind
  or trying to hold something with greased hands.

¹⁷ As iron sharpens iron,
       so a friend sharpens a friend.

¹⁸ As workers who tend a fig tree are allowed to
             eat the fruit,
         so workers who protect their employer's interests
             will be rewarded.

¹⁹ As a face is reflected in water,
       so the heart reflects the real person.

²⁰ Just as Death and Destruction are never satisfied,
       so human desire is never satisfied.

²¹ Fire tests the purity of silver and gold,
       but a person is tested by being praised.

²² You cannot separate fools from their foolishness,
       even though you grind them like grain with
           mortar and pestle.

²³ Know the state of your flocks,
       and put your heart into caring for your herds,
²⁴ for riches don't last forever,
       and the crown might not be passed to the next
           generation.
²⁵ After the hay is harvested and the new crop appears
       and the mountain grasses are gathered in,

²⁶ your sheep will provide wool for clothing,
    and your goats will provide the price of a field.
²⁷ And you will have enough goats' milk for yourself,
    your family, and your servant girls.

🌱 PSALM 130

A song for pilgrims ascending to Jerusalem.

1 From the depths of despair, O LORD,
 I call for your help.
2 Hear my cry, O Lord.
 Pay attention to my prayer.

3 LORD, if you kept a record of our sins,
 who, O Lord, could ever survive?
4 But you offer forgiveness,
 that we might learn to fear you.

5 I am counting on the LORD;
 yes, I am counting on him.
 I have put my hope in his word.
6 I long for the Lord
 more than sentries long for the dawn,
 yes, more than sentries long for the dawn.

7 O Israel, hope in the LORD;
 for with the LORD there is unfailing love.
 His redemption overflows.
8 He himself will redeem Israel
 from every kind of sin.

❦ PSALM 131

A song for pilgrims ascending to Jerusalem. A psalm of David.

1 LORD, my heart is not proud;
 my eyes are not haughty.
I don't concern myself with matters too great
 or too awesome for me to grasp.
2 Instead, I have calmed and quieted myself,
 like a weaned child who no longer cries for its
 mother's milk.
 Yes, like a weaned child is my soul within me.

3 O Israel, put your hope in the LORD—
 now and always.

❦ PSALM 132

A song for pilgrims ascending to Jerusalem.

1 LORD, remember David
 and all that he suffered.
2 He made a solemn promise to the LORD.
 He vowed to the Mighty One of Israel,
3 "I will not go home;
 I will not let myself rest.
4 I will not let my eyes sleep
 nor close my eyelids in slumber

⁵ until I find a place to build a house for
      the Lord,
      a sanctuary for the Mighty One of Israel."

⁶ We heard that the Ark was in Ephrathah;
      then we found it in the distant countryside
         of Jaar.
⁷ Let us go to the sanctuary of the Lord;
      let us worship at the footstool of his throne.
⁸ Arise, O Lord, and enter your resting place,
      along with the Ark, the symbol of your
         power.
⁹ May your priests be clothed in godliness;
      may your loyal servants sing for joy.
¹⁰ For the sake of your servant David,
      do not reject the king you have anointed.
¹¹ The Lord swore an oath to David
      with a promise he will never take back:
   "I will place one of your descendants
      on your throne.
¹² If your descendants obey the terms of
         my covenant
      and the laws that I teach them,
   then your royal line
      will continue forever and ever."

DAY 28   PSALM 132

¹³ For the Lord has chosen Jerusalem;
  he has desired it for his home.
¹⁴ "This is my resting place forever," he said.
  "I will live here, for this is the home I desired.
¹⁵ I will bless this city and make it prosperous;
  I will satisfy its poor with food.
¹⁶ I will clothe its priests with godliness;
  its faithful servants will sing for joy.
¹⁷ Here I will increase the power of David;
  my anointed one will be a light for my people.
¹⁸ I will clothe his enemies with shame,
  but he will be a glorious king."

❧ PSALM 133

A song for pilgrims ascending to Jerusalem. A psalm of David.

¹ How wonderful and pleasant it is
  when brothers live together in harmony!
² For harmony is as precious as the anointing oil
  that was poured over Aaron's head,
  that ran down his beard
  and onto the border of his robe.
³ Harmony is as refreshing as the dew from Mount
    Hermon
  that falls on the mountains of Zion.

And there the LORD has pronounced his blessing,
even life everlasting.

🕯 PSALM 134

A song for pilgrims ascending to Jerusalem.

1 Oh, praise the LORD, all you servants of the LORD,
you who serve at night in the house of the LORD.
2 Lift your hands toward the sanctuary,
and praise the LORD.

3 May the LORD, who made heaven and earth,
bless you from Jerusalem.

✳ PROVERBS 28

1 The wicked run away when no one is chasing them,
but the godly are as bold as lions.

2 When there is moral rot within a nation, its
government topples easily.
But wise and knowledgeable leaders bring
stability.

3 A poor person who oppresses the poor
is like a pounding rain that destroys the crops.

4 To reject the law is to praise the wicked;
to obey the law is to fight them.

⁵ Evil people don't understand justice,
  but those who follow the LORD understand
    completely.

⁶ Better to be poor and honest
  than to be dishonest and rich.

⁷ Young people who obey the law are wise;
  those with wild friends bring shame to their
    parents.

⁸ Income from charging high interest rates
  will end up in the pocket of someone who is
    kind to the poor.

⁹ God detests the prayers
  of a person who ignores the law.

¹⁰ Those who lead good people along an evil path
  will fall into their own trap,
  but the honest will inherit good things.

¹¹ Rich people may think they are wise,
  but a poor person with discernment can see right
    through them.

¹² When the godly succeed, everyone is glad.
  When the wicked take charge, people go into
    hiding.

¹³ People who conceal their sins will not prosper,
　　but if they confess and turn from them, they
　　　will receive mercy.

¹⁴ Blessed are those who fear to do wrong,
　　but the stubborn are headed for serious trouble.

¹⁵ A wicked ruler is as dangerous to the poor
　　as a roaring lion or an attacking bear.

¹⁶ A ruler with no understanding will oppress his
　　　people,
　　but one who hates corruption will have a
　　　long life.

¹⁷ A murderer's tormented conscience will drive
　　　him into the grave.
　　Don't protect him!

¹⁸ The blameless will be rescued from harm,
　　but the crooked will be suddenly destroyed.

¹⁹ A hard worker has plenty of food,
　　but a person who chases fantasies ends up in
　　　poverty.

²⁰ The trustworthy person will get a rich reward,
　　but a person who wants quick riches will get
　　　into trouble.

²¹ Showing partiality is never good,
yet some will do wrong for a mere piece of bread.

²² Greedy people try to get rich quick
but don't realize they're headed for poverty.

²³ In the end, people appreciate honest criticism
far more than flattery.

²⁴ Anyone who steals from his father and mother
and says, "What's wrong with that?"
is no better than a murderer.

²⁵ Greed causes fighting;
trusting the LORD leads to prosperity.

²⁶ Those who trust their own insight are foolish,
but anyone who walks in wisdom is safe.

²⁷ Whoever gives to the poor will lack nothing,
but those who close their eyes to poverty will
be cursed.

²⁸ When the wicked take charge, people go into
hiding.
When the wicked meet disaster, the godly
flourish.

DAY TWENTY-NINE

🔥 PSALM 135

¹ Praise the LORD!

Praise the name of the LORD!
  Praise him, you who serve the LORD,
² you who serve in the house of the LORD,
  in the courts of the house of our God.

³ Praise the LORD, for the LORD is good;
  celebrate his lovely name with music.
⁴ For the LORD has chosen Jacob for himself,
  Israel for his own special treasure.

⁵ I know the greatness of the LORD—
  that our Lord is greater than any other god.
⁶ The LORD does whatever pleases him
  throughout all heaven and earth,
  and on the seas and in their depths.
⁷ He causes the clouds to rise over the whole earth.
  He sends the lightning with the rain
  and releases the wind from his storehouses.

⁸ He destroyed the firstborn in each Egyptian home,
  both people and animals.

⁹ He performed miraculous signs and wonders
        in Egypt
    against Pharaoh and all his people.
¹⁰ He struck down great nations
    and slaughtered mighty kings—
¹¹ Sihon king of the Amorites,
        Og king of Bashan,
        and all the kings of Canaan.
¹² He gave their land as an inheritance,
    a special possession to his people Israel.

¹³ Your name, O LORD, endures forever;
    your fame, O LORD, is known to every
        generation.
¹⁴ For the LORD will give justice to his people
    and have compassion on his servants.

¹⁵ The idols of the nations are merely things
        of silver and gold,
    shaped by human hands.
¹⁶ They have mouths but cannot speak,
    and eyes but cannot see.
¹⁷ They have ears but cannot hear,
    and mouths but cannot breathe.
¹⁸ And those who make idols are just like them,
    as are all who trust in them.

¹⁹ O Israel, praise the LORD!
O priests—descendants of Aaron—praise the
LORD!
²⁰ O Levites, praise the LORD!
All you who fear the LORD, praise the LORD!
²¹ The LORD be praised from Zion,
for he lives here in Jerusalem.

Praise the LORD!

❦ PSALM 136

¹ Give thanks to the LORD, for he is good!
His faithful love endures forever.
² Give thanks to the God of gods.
His faithful love endures forever.
³ Give thanks to the Lord of lords.
His faithful love endures forever.

⁴ Give thanks to him who alone does mighty miracles.
His faithful love endures forever.
⁵ Give thanks to him who made the heavens so
skillfully.
His faithful love endures forever.
⁶ Give thanks to him who placed the earth among
the waters.
His faithful love endures forever.

7 Give thanks to him who made the heavenly lights—
His faithful love endures forever.

8 the sun to rule the day,
His faithful love endures forever.

9 and the moon and stars to rule the night.
His faithful love endures forever.

10 Give thanks to him who killed the firstborn of Egypt.
His faithful love endures forever.

11 He brought Israel out of Egypt.
His faithful love endures forever.

12 He acted with a strong hand and powerful arm.
His faithful love endures forever.

13 Give thanks to him who parted the Red Sea.
His faithful love endures forever.

14 He led Israel safely through,
His faithful love endures forever.

15 but he hurled Pharaoh and his army into the Red Sea.
His faithful love endures forever.

16 Give thanks to him who led his people through
the wilderness.
His faithful love endures forever.

17 Give thanks to him who struck down mighty kings.
His faithful love endures forever.

¹⁸ He killed powerful kings—

> *His faithful love endures forever.*

¹⁹ Sihon king of the Amorites,

> *His faithful love endures forever.*

²⁰ and Og king of Bashan.

> *His faithful love endures forever.*

²¹ God gave the land of these kings as an
inheritance—

> *His faithful love endures forever.*

²² a special possession to his servant Israel.

> *His faithful love endures forever.*

²³ He remembered us in our weakness.

> *His faithful love endures forever.*

²⁴ He saved us from our enemies.

> *His faithful love endures forever.*

²⁵ He gives food to every living thing.

> *His faithful love endures forever.*

²⁶ Give thanks to the God of heaven.

> *His faithful love endures forever.*

❧ PSALM 137

¹ Beside the rivers of Babylon, we sat and wept
as we thought of Jerusalem.

² We put away our harps,

  hanging them on the branches of poplar trees.

³ For our captors demanded a song from us.

  Our tormentors insisted on a joyful hymn:

  "Sing us one of those songs of Jerusalem!"

⁴ But how can we sing the songs of the LORD

  while in a pagan land?

⁵ If I forget you, O Jerusalem,

  let my right hand forget how to play

    the harp.

⁶ May my tongue stick to the roof of my mouth

  if I fail to remember you,

  if I don't make Jerusalem my greatest joy.

⁷ O LORD, remember what the Edomites did

  on the day the armies of Babylon captured

    Jerusalem.

 "Destroy it!" they yelled.

  "Level it to the ground!"

⁸ O Babylon, you will be destroyed.

  Happy is the one who pays you back

  for what you have done to us.

⁹ Happy is the one who takes your babies

  and smashes them against the rocks!

# PSALM 138

A psalm of David.

¹ I give you thanks, O Lord, with all my heart;
    I will sing your praises before the gods.
² I bow before your holy Temple as I worship.
        I praise your name for your unfailing love and
            faithfulness;
    for your promises are backed
        by all the honor of your name.
³ As soon as I pray, you answer me;
        you encourage me by giving me strength.

⁴ Every king in all the earth will thank you, Lord,
        for all of them will hear your words.
⁵ Yes, they will sing about the Lord's ways,
        for the glory of the Lord is very great.
⁶ Though the Lord is great, he cares for
            the humble,
        but he keeps his distance from the proud.

⁷ Though I am surrounded by troubles,
        you will protect me from the anger of my
            enemies.
    You reach out your hand,
        and the power of your right hand saves me.

8 The LORD will work out his plans for my life—
  for your faithful love, O LORD, endures forever.
  Don't abandon me, for you made me.

🔥 PSALM 139
For the choir director: A psalm of David.

1 O LORD, you have examined my heart
  and know everything about me.
2 You know when I sit down or stand up.
  You know my thoughts even when I'm
    far away.
3 You see me when I travel
  and when I rest at home.
  You know everything I do.
4 You know what I am going to say
  even before I say it, LORD.
5 You go before me and follow me.
  You place your hand of blessing on my head.
6 Such knowledge is too wonderful for me,
  too great for me to understand!

7 I can never escape from your Spirit!
  I can never get away from your presence!
8 If I go up to heaven, you are there;
  if I go down to the grave, you are there.

⁹ If I ride the wings of the morning,
    if I dwell by the farthest oceans,
¹⁰ even there your hand will guide me,
    and your strength will support me.
¹¹ I could ask the darkness to hide me
    and the light around me to become night—
¹²   but even in darkness I cannot hide from you.
  To you the night shines as bright as day.
    Darkness and light are the same to you.

¹³ You made all the delicate, inner parts of my body
    and knit me together in my mother's womb.
¹⁴ Thank you for making me so wonderfully complex!
    Your workmanship is marvelous—how well I
        know it.
¹⁵ You watched me as I was being formed in utter
        seclusion,
    as I was woven together in the dark of the womb.
¹⁶ You saw me before I was born.
    Every day of my life was recorded in your book.
  Every moment was laid out
    before a single day had passed.

¹⁷ How precious are your thoughts about me, O God.
    They cannot be numbered!

¹⁸ I can't even count them;
   they outnumber the grains of sand!
And when I wake up,
   you are still with me!

¹⁹ O God, if only you would destroy the wicked!
   Get out of my life, you murderers!
²⁰ They blaspheme you;
   your enemies misuse your name.
²¹ O LORD, shouldn't I hate those who hate you?
   Shouldn't I despise those who oppose you?
²² Yes, I hate them with total hatred,
   for your enemies are my enemies.

²³ Search me, O God, and know my heart;
   test me and know my anxious thoughts.
²⁴ Point out anything in me that offends you,
   and lead me along the path of everlasting life.

✳ PROVERBS 29

¹ Whoever stubbornly refuses to accept criticism
   will suddenly be destroyed beyond recovery.

² When the godly are in authority, the people
   rejoice.
   But when the wicked are in power, they groan.

³ The man who loves wisdom brings joy to
     his father,
    but if he hangs around with prostitutes, his
     wealth is wasted.

⁴ A just king gives stability to his nation,
    but one who demands bribes destroys it.

⁵ To flatter friends
    is to lay a trap for their feet.

⁶ Evil people are trapped by sin,
    but the righteous escape, shouting for joy.

⁷ The godly care about the rights of the poor;
    the wicked don't care at all.

⁸ Mockers can get a whole town agitated,
    but the wise will calm anger.

⁹ If a wise person takes a fool to court,
    there will be ranting and ridicule but no
     satisfaction.

¹⁰ The bloodthirsty hate blameless people,
    but the upright seek to help them.

¹¹ Fools vent their anger,
    but the wise quietly hold it back.

¹² If a ruler pays attention to liars,
all his advisers will be wicked.

¹³ The poor and the oppressor have this in common—
the Lord gives sight to the eyes of both.

¹⁴ If a king judges the poor fairly,
his throne will last forever.

¹⁵ To discipline a child produces wisdom,
but a mother is disgraced by an undisciplined
child.

¹⁶ When the wicked are in authority, sin flourishes,
but the godly will live to see their downfall.

¹⁷ Discipline your children, and they will give you
peace of mind
and will make your heart glad.

¹⁸ When people do not accept divine guidance, they
run wild.
But whoever obeys the law is joyful.

¹⁹ Words alone will not discipline a servant;
the words may be understood, but they are not
heeded.

²⁰ There is more hope for a fool
than for someone who speaks without thinking.

²¹ A servant pampered from childhood
     will become a rebel.

²² An angry person starts fights;
     a hot-tempered person commits all kinds of sin.

²³ Pride ends in humiliation,
     while humility brings honor.

²⁴ If you assist a thief, you only hurt yourself.
     You are sworn to tell the truth, but you dare
        not testify.

²⁵ Fearing people is a dangerous trap,
     but trusting the LORD means safety.

²⁶ Many seek the ruler's favor,
     but justice comes from the LORD.

²⁷ The righteous despise the unjust;
     the wicked despise the godly.

DAY THIRTY

🕯 PSALM 140

For the choir director: A psalm of David.

¹ O Lord, rescue me from evil people.
    Protect me from those who are violent,
² those who plot evil in their hearts
    and stir up trouble all day long.
³ Their tongues sting like a snake;
    the venom of a viper drips from their lips.

Interlude

⁴ O Lord, keep me out of the hands of the wicked.
    Protect me from those who are violent,
    for they are plotting against me.
⁵ The proud have set a trap to catch me;
    they have stretched out a net;
    they have placed traps all along the way.

Interlude

⁶ I said to the Lord, "You are my God!"
    Listen, O Lord, to my cries for mercy!
⁷ O Sovereign Lord, the strong one who
        rescued me,
    you protected me on the day of battle.

⁸ LORD, do not let evil people have their way.
    Do not let their evil schemes succeed,
        or they will become proud.   *Interlude*

⁹ Let my enemies be destroyed
    by the very evil they have planned for me.
¹⁰ Let burning coals fall down on their heads.
    Let them be thrown into the fire
        or into watery pits from which they can't escape.
¹¹ Don't let liars prosper here in our land.
    Cause great disasters to fall on the violent.

¹² But I know the LORD will help those they persecute;
    he will give justice to the poor.
¹³ Surely righteous people are praising your name;
    the godly will live in your presence.

❦ PSALM 141
A psalm of David.

¹ O LORD, I am calling to you. Please hurry!
    Listen when I cry to you for help!
² Accept my prayer as incense offered to you,
    and my upraised hands as an evening offering.

³ Take control of what I say, O LORD,
    and guard my lips.

⁴ Don't let me drift toward evil
    or take part in acts of wickedness.
Don't let me share in the delicacies
    of those who do wrong.

⁵ Let the godly strike me!
    It will be a kindness!
If they correct me, it is soothing medicine.
    Don't let me refuse it.

But I pray constantly
    against the wicked and their deeds.
⁶ When their leaders are thrown down from
        a cliff,
    the wicked will listen to my words and
        find them true.
⁷ Like rocks brought up by a plow,
    the bones of the wicked will lie scattered
        without burial.

⁸ I look to you for help, O Sovereign LORD.
    You are my refuge; don't let them kill me.
⁹ Keep me from the traps they have set for me,
    from the snares of those who do wrong.
¹⁰ Let the wicked fall into their own nets,
    but let me escape.

❦ PSALM 142

A psalm of David, regarding his experience in the cave. A prayer.

¹ I cry out to the LORD;
  I plead for the LORD's mercy.
² I pour out my complaints before him
  and tell him all my troubles.
³ When I am overwhelmed,
  you alone know the way I should turn.
 Wherever I go,
  my enemies have set traps for me.
⁴ I look for someone to come and help me,
  but no one gives me a passing thought!
 No one will help me;
  no one cares a bit what happens to me.
⁵ Then I pray to you, O LORD.
  I say, "You are my place of refuge.
  You are all I really want in life.
⁶ Hear my cry,
  for I am very low.
 Rescue me from my persecutors,
  for they are too strong for me.
⁷ Bring me out of prison
  so I can thank you.
 The godly will crowd around me,
  for you are good to me."

🔥 PSALM 143

A psalm of David.

¹ Hear my prayer, O LORD;
    listen to my plea!
    Answer me because you are faithful and
        righteous.
² Don't put your servant on trial,
    for no one is innocent before you.
³ My enemy has chased me.
    He has knocked me to the ground
    and forces me to live in darkness like those
        in the grave.
⁴ I am losing all hope;
    I am paralyzed with fear.
⁵ I remember the days of old.
    I ponder all your great works
    and think about what you have done.
⁶ I lift my hands to you in prayer.
    I thirst for you as parched land thirsts for rain.

Interlude

⁷ Come quickly, LORD, and answer me,
    for my depression deepens.
  Don't turn away from me,
    or I will die.

[8] Let me hear of your unfailing love each morning,
  for I am trusting you.
Show me where to walk,
  for I give myself to you.
[9] Rescue me from my enemies, LORD;
  I run to you to hide me.
[10] Teach me to do your will,
  for you are my God.
May your gracious Spirit lead me forward
  on a firm footing.
[11] For the glory of your name, O LORD, preserve
  my life.
  Because of your faithfulness, bring me out
    of this distress.
[12] In your unfailing love, silence all my enemies
  and destroy all my foes,
  for I am your servant.

❧ PSALM 144

A psalm of David.

[1] Praise the LORD, who is my rock.
  He trains my hands for war
  and gives my fingers skill for battle.
[2] He is my loving ally and my fortress,
  my tower of safety, my rescuer.

He is my shield, and I take refuge in him.
  He makes the nations submit to me.

³ O Lord, what are human beings that you should
    notice them,
  mere mortals that you should think about them?
⁴ For they are like a breath of air;
  their days are like a passing shadow.

⁵ Open the heavens, Lord, and come down.
  Touch the mountains so they billow smoke.
⁶ Hurl your lightning bolts and scatter your enemies!
  Shoot your arrows and confuse them!
⁷ Reach down from heaven and rescue me;
  rescue me from deep waters,
  from the power of my enemies.
⁸ Their mouths are full of lies;
  they swear to tell the truth, but they lie instead.

⁹ I will sing a new song to you, O God!
  I will sing your praises with a ten-stringed harp.
¹⁰ For you grant victory to kings!
  You rescued your servant David from the fatal
    sword.
¹¹ Save me!
  Rescue me from the power of my enemies.

Their mouths are full of lies;
    they swear to tell the truth, but they lie instead.

12 May our sons flourish in their youth
    like well-nurtured plants.
May our daughters be like graceful pillars,
    carved to beautify a palace.
13 May our barns be filled
    with crops of every kind.
May the flocks in our fields multiply by the
      thousands,
    even tens of thousands,
14   and may our oxen be loaded down with produce.
May there be no enemy breaking through our walls,
    no going into captivity,
    no cries of alarm in our town squares.
15 Yes, joyful are those who live like this!
    Joyful indeed are those whose God is the LORD.

✳ PROVERBS 30

The sayings of Agur son of Jakeh contain this
message.

    I am weary, O God;
      I am weary and worn out, O God.

² I am too stupid to be human,
   and I lack common sense.
³ I have not mastered human wisdom,
   nor do I know the Holy One.

⁴ Who but God goes up to heaven and comes
      back down?
   Who holds the wind in his fists?
 Who wraps up the oceans in his cloak?
   Who has created the whole wide world?
 What is his name—and his son's name?
   Tell me if you know!

⁵ Every word of God proves true.
   He is a shield to all who come to him for
      protection.
⁶ Do not add to his words,
   or he may rebuke you and expose you as a liar.

⁷ O God, I beg two favors from you;
   let me have them before I die.
⁸ First, help me never to tell a lie.
   Second, give me neither poverty nor riches!
   Give me just enough to satisfy my needs.
⁹ For if I grow rich, I may deny you and say,
   "Who is the LORD?"

And if I am too poor, I may steal and thus insult
   God's holy name.

10 Never slander a worker to the employer,
   or the person will curse you, and you will pay
      for it.

11 Some people curse their father
   and do not thank their mother.
12 They are pure in their own eyes,
   but they are filthy and unwashed.
13 They look proudly around,
   casting disdainful glances.
14 They have teeth like swords
   and fangs like knives.
   They devour the poor from the earth
   and the needy from among humanity.

15 The leech has two suckers
   that cry out, "More, more!"

There are three things that are never satisfied—
   no, four that never say, "Enough!":
16 the grave,
   the barren womb,
   the thirsty desert,
   the blazing fire.

¹⁷ The eye that mocks a father
　　and despises a mother's instructions
　will be plucked out by ravens of the valley
　　and eaten by vultures.

¹⁸ There are three things that amaze me—
　　no, four things that I don't understand:
¹⁹ how an eagle glides through the sky,
　　how a snake slithers on a rock,
　　how a ship navigates the ocean,
　　how a man loves a woman.

²⁰ An adulterous woman consumes a man,
　　then wipes her mouth and says, "What's wrong
　　　with that?"

²¹ There are three things that make the earth tremble—
　　no, four it cannot endure:
²² a slave who becomes a king,
　　an overbearing fool who prospers,
²³ 　a bitter woman who finally gets a husband,
　　a servant girl who supplants her mistress.

²⁴ There are four things on earth that are small but
　　　unusually wise:
²⁵ Ants—they aren't strong,
　　but they store up food all summer.

²⁶ Hyraxes—they aren't powerful,
   but they make their homes among the rocks.
²⁷ Locusts—they have no king,
   but they march in formation.
²⁸ Lizards—they are easy to catch,
   but they are found even in kings' palaces.

²⁹ There are three things that walk with stately
      stride—
   no, four that strut about:
³⁰ the lion, king of animals, who won't turn aside
      for anything,
³¹   the strutting rooster,
   the male goat,
   a king as he leads his army.

³² If you have been a fool by being proud or
      plotting evil,
   cover your mouth in shame.

³³ As the beating of cream yields butter
   and striking the nose causes bleeding,
 · so stirring up anger causes quarrels.

DAY THIRTY-ONE

❦ PSALM 145
A psalm of praise of David.

¹ I will exalt you, my God and King,
    and praise your name forever and ever.
² I will praise you every day;
    yes, I will praise you forever.
³ Great is the LORD! He is most worthy of praise!
    No one can measure his greatness.

⁴ Let each generation tell its children of your
        mighty acts;
    let them proclaim your power.
⁵ I will meditate on your majestic, glorious
        splendor
    and your wonderful miracles.
⁶ Your awe-inspiring deeds will be on every tongue;
    I will proclaim your greatness.
⁷ Everyone will share the story of your wonderful
        goodness;
    they will sing with joy about your righteousness.

⁸ The LORD is merciful and compassionate,
    slow to get angry and filled with unfailing love.

⁹ The LORD is good to everyone.
   He showers compassion on all his creation.
¹⁰ All of your works will thank you, LORD,
   and your faithful followers will praise you.
¹¹ They will speak of the glory of your kingdom;
   they will give examples of your power.
¹² They will tell about your mighty deeds
   and about the majesty and glory of your reign.
¹³ For your kingdom is an everlasting kingdom.
   You rule throughout all generations.

   The LORD always keeps his promises;
   he is gracious in all he does.
¹⁴ The LORD helps the fallen
   and lifts those bent beneath their loads.
¹⁵ The eyes of all look to you in hope;
   you give them their food as they need it.
¹⁶ When you open your hand,
   you satisfy the hunger and thirst of every
      living thing.
¹⁷ The LORD is righteous in everything he does;
   he is filled with kindness.
¹⁸ The LORD is close to all who call on him,
   yes, to all who call on him in truth.

¹⁹ He grants the desires of those who fear him;
    he hears their cries for help and rescues them.
²⁰ The LORD protects all those who love him,
    but he destroys the wicked.

²¹ I will praise the LORD,
    and may everyone on earth bless his
      holy name
    forever and ever.

🔥 PSALM 146

¹ Praise the LORD!

Let all that I am praise the LORD.
²   I will praise the LORD as long as I live.
    I will sing praises to my God with my dying
      breath.

³ Don't put your confidence in powerful people;
    there is no help for you there.
⁴ When they breathe their last, they return to the
      earth,
    and all their plans die with them.
⁵ But joyful are those who have the God of Israel
      as their helper,
    whose hope is in the LORD their God.

⁶ He made heaven and earth,
    the sea, and everything in them.
    He keeps every promise forever.
⁷ He gives justice to the oppressed
    and food to the hungry.
  The LORD frees the prisoners.
⁸   The LORD opens the eyes of the blind.
  The LORD lifts up those who are weighed down.
    The LORD loves the godly.
⁹ The LORD protects the foreigners among us.
    He cares for the orphans and widows,
    but he frustrates the plans of the wicked.

¹⁰ The LORD will reign forever.
    He will be your God, O Jerusalem, throughout
      the generations.

  Praise the LORD!

❧ PSALM 147

¹ Praise the LORD!

  How good to sing praises to our God!
    How delightful and how fitting!
² The LORD is rebuilding Jerusalem
    and bringing the exiles back to Israel.

³ He heals the brokenhearted
    and bandages their wounds.
⁴ He counts the stars
    and calls them all by name.
⁵ How great is our Lord! His power is absolute!
    His understanding is beyond comprehension!
⁶ The LORD supports the humble,
    but he brings the wicked down into the dust.

⁷ Sing out your thanks to the LORD;
    sing praises to our God with a harp.
⁸ He covers the heavens with clouds,
    provides rain for the earth,
    and makes the grass grow in mountain pastures.
⁹ He gives food to the wild animals
    and feeds the young ravens when they cry.
¹⁰ He takes no pleasure in the strength of a horse
    or in human might.
¹¹ No, the LORD's delight is in those who fear him,
    those who put their hope in his unfailing love.

¹² Glorify the LORD, O Jerusalem!
    Praise your God, O Zion!
¹³ For he has strengthened the bars of your gates
    and blessed your children within your walls.

¹⁴ He sends peace across your nation
and satisfies your hunger with the finest
wheat.
¹⁵ He sends his orders to the world—
how swiftly his word flies!
¹⁶ He sends the snow like white wool;
he scatters frost upon the ground like ashes.
¹⁷ He hurls the hail like stones.
Who can stand against his freezing cold?
¹⁸ Then, at his command, it all melts.
He sends his winds, and the ice thaws.
¹⁹ He has revealed his words to Jacob,
his decrees and regulations to Israel.
²⁰ He has not done this for any other nation;
they do not know his regulations.

Praise the LORD!

❧ PSALM 148

¹ Praise the LORD!

Praise the LORD from the heavens!
Praise him from the skies!
² Praise him, all his angels!
Praise him, all the armies of heaven!

3 Praise him, sun and moon!
  Praise him, all you twinkling stars!
4 Praise him, skies above!
  Praise him, vapors high above the clouds!
5 Let every created thing give praise to the LORD,
  for he issued his command, and they came
    into being.
6 He set them in place forever and ever.
  His decree will never be revoked.

7 Praise the LORD from the earth,
  you creatures of the ocean depths,
8 fire and hail, snow and clouds,
  wind and weather that obey him,
9 mountains and all hills,
  fruit trees and all cedars,
10 wild animals and all livestock,
  small scurrying animals and birds,
11 kings of the earth and all people,
  rulers and judges of the earth,
12 young men and young women,
  old men and children.

13 Let them all praise the name of the LORD.
  For his name is very great;
  his glory towers over the earth and heaven!

¹⁴ He has made his people strong,
  honoring his faithful ones—
  the people of Israel who are close to him.

Praise the LORD!

🌿 PSALM 149

¹ Praise the LORD!

Sing to the LORD a new song.
  Sing his praises in the assembly of the faithful.

² O Israel, rejoice in your Maker.
  O people of Jerusalem, exult in your King.
³ Praise his name with dancing,
  accompanied by tambourine and harp.
⁴ For the LORD delights in his people;
  he crowns the humble with victory.
⁵ Let the faithful rejoice that he honors them.
  Let them sing for joy as they lie on their beds.

⁶ Let the praises of God be in their mouths,
  and a sharp sword in their hands—
⁷ to execute vengeance on the nations
  and punishment on the peoples,
⁸ to bind their kings with shackles
  and their leaders with iron chains,

⁹ to execute the judgment written against them.
This is the glorious privilege of his faithful ones.

Praise the LORD!

🕯 PSALM 150

¹ Praise the LORD!

Praise God in his sanctuary;
praise him in his mighty heaven!
² Praise him for his mighty works;
praise his unequaled greatness!
³ Praise him with a blast of the ram's horn;
praise him with the lyre and harp!
⁴ Praise him with the tambourine and dancing;
praise him with strings and flutes!
⁵ Praise him with a clash of cymbals;
praise him with loud clanging cymbals.
⁶ Let everything that breathes sing praises to the
LORD!

Praise the LORD!

✳ PROVERBS 31

The sayings of King Lemuel contain this message,
which his mother taught him.

² O my son, O son of my womb,
　　O son of my vows,
³ do not waste your strength on women,
　　on those who ruin kings.

⁴ It is not for kings, O Lemuel, to guzzle wine.
　　Rulers should not crave alcohol.
⁵ For if they drink, they may forget the law
　　and not give justice to the oppressed.
⁶ Alcohol is for the dying,
　　and wine for those in bitter distress.
⁷ Let them drink to forget their poverty
　　and remember their troubles no more.

⁸ Speak up for those who cannot speak for
　　　themselves;
　　ensure justice for those being crushed.
⁹ Yes, speak up for the poor and helpless,
　　and see that they get justice.

¹⁰ Who can find a virtuous and capable wife?
　　She is more precious than rubies.
¹¹ Her husband can trust her,
　　and she will greatly enrich his life.
¹² She brings him good, not harm,
　　all the days of her life.

¹³ She finds wool and flax
  and busily spins it.
¹⁴ She is like a merchant's ship,
  bringing her food from afar.
¹⁵ She gets up before dawn to prepare breakfast for
    her household
  and plan the day's work for her servant girls.

¹⁶ She goes to inspect a field and buys it;
  with her earnings she plants a vineyard.
¹⁷ She is energetic and strong,
  a hard worker.
¹⁸ She makes sure her dealings are profitable;
  her lamp burns late into the night.

¹⁹ Her hands are busy spinning thread,
  her fingers twisting fiber.
²⁰ She extends a helping hand to the poor
  and opens her arms to the needy.
²¹ She has no fear of winter for her household,
  for everyone has warm clothes.

²² She makes her own bedspreads.
  She dresses in fine linen and purple gowns.
²³ Her husband is well known at the city gates,
  where he sits with the other civic leaders.

[24] She makes belted linen garments
   and sashes to sell to the merchants.
[25] She is clothed with strength and dignity,
   and she laughs without fear of the future.
[26] When she speaks, her words are wise,
   and she gives instructions with kindness.
[27] She carefully watches everything in her household
   and suffers nothing from laziness.

[28] Her children stand and bless her.
   Her husband praises her:
[29] "There are many virtuous and capable women in
      the world,
   but you surpass them all!"

[30] Charm is deceptive, and beauty does not last;
   but a woman who fears the LORD will be greatly
      praised.
[31] Reward her for all she has done.
   Let her deeds publicly declare her praise.

🌱 PSALMS

When the eleven disciples were gathered behind locked doors on the night of Christ's resurrection, we are told that they were greatly disturbed and fearful. Then the Lord entered the room and said to them, "Peace be with you" (Luke 24:36). What He brought to the disciples He can bring to the mind and heart of any individual who will let Him in.

Jesus began His discourse to the disciples by saying, "Why are you frightened? . . . Look at my hands. Look at my feet. You can see that it's really me. Touch me and make sure that I am not a ghost, because ghosts don't have bodies, as you see that I do." Then he turned to them and said, "Do you have anything here to eat?" Jesus concluded by saying, "When I was with you before, I told you that everything written about me in the law of Moses and the prophets and in the Psalms must be fulfilled." And Luke adds:

"Then he opened their minds to understand the Scriptures" (24:38-45).

Thus it is on the authority of the Lord Jesus Christ Himself that we are to find Christ in the Psalms. No one can properly understand the Cross or fathom why Jesus endured its agony without having studied the Psalms. For example, when we read Luke 24, we see its relationship to Psalm 1. The first three verses of Psalm 1 convey that the one who does not follow the advice of the wicked is blessed and happy.

> "Oh, the joys of those who do not follow
> the advice of the wicked, . . . or join in
> with mockers. But they delight in the law
> of the LORD; meditating on it day and
> night. They are like trees planted along the
> riverbank, bearing fruit each season. Their
> leaves never wither, and they prosper in all
> they do."

The only one who could experience this completely is the Lord Jesus Christ, for He is the only one who never walked in the counsel of the ungodly.

While the first three verses of Psalm 1 speak particularly of Christ, the one who believes in Christ can also describe his or her position with the Lord in terms of these verses. Certainly there is no true and lasting happiness in this world today apart from the Blessed One, that is to say, apart from the Lord Jesus Christ.

✳ PROVERBS

Of all inspired thoughts in the book of Proverbs, the key statement is found in chapter 3, verses 13-14: "Joyful is the person who finds wisdom, and the one who gains understanding. For wisdom is more profitable than silver, and her wages are better than gold." When we read God's Word, it is God speaking to people. When Christians pray, it is people speaking to God.

In the Psalms, Christians are found on their knees. In the book of Proverbs, Christians are found on their feet doing things. The Psalms are for devotion; the Proverbs are for the Christian's walk and warfare. The Proverbs are for the businessperson, for the layperson, for young people in their everyday walk and life, and for the church leader.

In the opening verse of the book of Proverbs, we read the superscription, "These are the proverbs of Solomon, David's son, king of Israel." We are told that what follows is given for our wisdom and instruction. Solomon was a great scientist and philosopher. He was also the architect of one of the wonders of the ancient world, the temple in Jerusalem. He was also a king. In 1 Kings 4:29, we read that "God gave Solomon very great wisdom and understanding, and knowledge as vast as the sands of the seashore."

Solomon gathered sayings given by the Holy Spirit, arranged them in an orderly fashion, and preserved them for us and our daily instruction.

In the first ten chapters of Proverbs, we find counsel for young people. The second ten provide counsel for people in all stages of life. The next chapters, 21–30, are counsel for kings and rulers, and the book closes with chapter 31, a beautiful description of women's rights.

May you find much joy and strength in your reading, and may you find, as Solomon did, that "Timely advice is lovely, like golden apples in a silver basket" (Proverbs 25:11).

George M. Wilson

FIND HELP IN THE PSALMS AND PROVERBS

Read These Psalms When You . . . .

Feel troubled *17, 20, 23, 27, 28, 40, 43, 54, 57, 62, 63, 64, 67, 86*

Feel persecuted *56, 59, 69, 70, 102, 140, 141, 142, 143*

Feel "cornered" *36, 68*

Feel things have "gone sour" *42*

Feel like complaining *39*

Feel envious of people *73*

Feel your friends have turned against you *35, 41, 55*

Need assurance *3*

Are angry with someone *133*

Have sinned *32, 51, 79, 80, 106, 130*

Need help *38, 83*

Are facing important decisions *25, 26, 91*

Are troubled by godlessness in the world *2, 9, 46, 52, 75, 76*

Need encouragement as a senior citizen *71*

Feel timid about sharing your faith *67*

Have responsibility in governing others *21, 72, 82, 94*

Find it difficult to be thankful *66*

Need to get your mind off yourself and praise God *92, 96, 97, 98, 100, 117, 136, 138, 139, 145, 147, 148, 150*

These Psalms Will Remind You that . . . .

God and one are a majority *18*

God is worth trusting *4, 29, 33, 34, 65, 99, 118*

God loves His own *8, 31, 81, 91, 105, 106, 111, 121, 149*

God hears our prayers *103, 108, 116*

God is alive *8, 14, 84, 115*

God is in control of history *24, 45, 47, 87, 99, 110, 124, 135*

Highlights in Proverbs on the Subjects of . . . .

Steps to Peace With God

STEP 1 **God's Purpose: Peace and Life**

God loves you and wants you
to experience peace and
life—abundant and eternal.

THE BIBLE SAYS ...

*"We have peace with God through
our Lord Jesus Christ."*
Romans 5:1, NIV

*"For God so loved the world that
He gave His only begotten Son, that
whoever believes in Him should not
perish but have everlasting life."*
John 3:16, NKJV

*"I have come that they may have
life, and that they may have it more
abundantly."* John 10:10, NKJV

Since God
planned for
us to have
peace and the
abundant life
right now,
why are most
people not
having this
experience?

STEP 2 **Our Problem: Separation From God**

God created us in His own image to have an abundant life. He did not make us as robots to automatically love and obey Him, but gave us a will and a freedom of choice.

We chose to disobey God and go our own willful way. We still make this choice today. This results in separation from God.

THE BIBLE SAYS ...

"For all have sinned and fall short of the glory of God."
Romans 3:23, NIV

"For the wages of sin is death, but the gift of God is eternal life in Christ Jesus our Lord." Romans 6:23, NIV

Our choice
results
in separation
from God.

Our Attempts

Through the ages, individuals have tried in many ways to bridge this gap ... without success ...

THE BIBLE SAYS ...

"*There is a way that appears to be right, but in the end it leads to death.*" Proverbs 14:12, NIV

"*But your iniquities have separated you from your God; and your sins have hidden His face from you, so that He will not hear.*" Isaiah 59:2, NKJV

There is only one remedy for this problem of separation.

STEP 3   God's Remedy: The Cross

Jesus Christ is the only answer to this problem. He died on the cross and rose from the grave, paying the penalty for our sin and bridging the gap between God and people.

THE BIBLE SAYS ...

"For there is one God and one mediator between God and mankind, the man Christ Jesus."
1 Timothy 2:5, NIV

"For Christ also suffered once for sins, the just for the unjust, that He might bring us to God."
1 Peter 3:18, NKJV

"But God demonstrates his own love for us in this: While we were still sinners, Christ died for us."
Romans 5:8, NIV

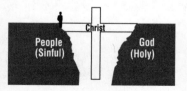

God has provided the only way ... we must make the choice ...

STEP 4 **Our Response: Receive Christ**

We must trust Jesus Christ and receive Him by
personal invitation ...

THE BIBLE SAYS ...

*"Behold, I stand at the door and knock. If anyone
hears My voice and opens the door, I will come in
to him and dine with him, and he with Me."*
Revelation 3:20, NKJV

*"But as many as received Him, to them He gave the
right to become children of God, to those who believe in
His name."* John 1:12, NKJV

*"If you confess with your mouth the Lord Jesus and
believe in your heart that God has raised Him from
the dead, you will be saved."* Romans 10:9, NKJV

Are you here ...   or here?

Is there any good reason why you cannot receive Jesus Christ right now?

How to receive Christ:

1. Admit your need. (I am a sinner.)
2. Be willing to turn from your sins (repent).
3. Believe that Jesus Christ died for you on the cross and rose from the grave.
4. Through prayer, invite Jesus Christ to come in and control your life through the Holy Spirit. (Receive Him as Lord and Savior.)

What to Pray:

Dear Lord Jesus,
I know that I am a sinner, and I ask for Your forgiveness. I believe You died for my sins and rose from the dead. I turn from my sins and invite You to come into my heart and life. I want to trust and follow You as my Lord and Savior.
In Your Name, amen.

_____ _____
Date   Signature

God's Assurance: His Word

If you prayed this prayer,

THE BIBLE SAYS ...

"For 'whoever calls on the name of the Lord shall be saved.'" Romans 10:13, NKJV

Did you sincerely ask Jesus Christ to come into your life? Where is He right now? What has He given you?

"For it is by grace you have been saved, through faith—and this is not from yourselves, it is the gift of God—not by works, so that no one can boast." Ephesians 2:8–9, NIV

The Bible Says ...

"He who has the Son has life; he who does not have the Son of God does not have life. These things I have written to you who believe in the name of the Son of God, that you may know that you have eternal life, and that you may continue to believe in the name of the Son of God." 1 John 5:12–13, NKJV

Receiving Christ, we are born into God's family through the supernatural work of the Holy Spirit who indwells every believer. This is called regeneration or the "new birth."

This is just the beginning of a wonderful new life in Christ. To deepen this relationship, you should:
1. Read your Bible every day to know Christ better.
2. Talk to God in prayer every day.
3. Tell others about Christ.
4. Worship, fellowship, and serve with other Christians in a church where Christ is preached.
5. As Christ's representative in a needy world, demonstrate your new life by your love and concern for others.

God bless you as you do.
Billy Graham

If you are committing your life to Christ, please let us know!

We would like to send you Bible study materials to help you grow in your faith.

The Billy Graham Evangelistic Association exists to support and extend the evangelistic calling and ministries of Billy Graham and Franklin Graham by proclaiming the Gospel of the Lord Jesus Christ to all we can by every effective means available to us and by equipping others to do the same.

Our desire is to introduce as many people as we can to the person of Jesus Christ, so that they might experience His love and forgiveness.

Your prayers are the most important way to support us in this ministry. We are grateful for the dedicated prayer support we receive. We are also grateful for those who support us with financial contributions.

Billy Graham Evangelistic Association
1 Billy Graham Parkway
Charlotte, North Carolina 28201-0001
BillyGraham.org
Toll-free: 1-877-2GRAHAM
(1-877-247-2426)

Billy Graham Evangelistic Association of Canada
20 Hopewell Way NE
Calgary, Alberta T3J 5H5
BillyGraham.ca
Toll-free: 1-888-393-0003

Notes

_____

_____

_____

_____

_____

_____

_____

_____

_____

_____

_____

_____

_____

Notes

Notes

Notes

Notes

Notes